Poverty in Britain

Poverty in Britain

The impact of government policy since 1997

Holly Sutherland, Tom Sefton and David Piachaud

JOSEPH ROWNTREE FOUNDATION

The **Joseph Rowntree Foundation** has supported this project as part of its programme of research and innovative development projects, which it hopes will be of value to policy makers, practitioners and service users. The facts presented and views expressed in this report are, however, those of the authors and not necessarily those of the Foundation.

Joseph Rowntree Foundation
The Homestead
40 Water End
York YO30 6WP
Website: www.jrf.org.uk

About the authors
Holly Sutherland is Director of the Microsimulation Unit in the Department of Applied Economics at the University of Cambridge. Tom Sefton is Research Fellow at the ESRC Research Centre for Analysis of Social Exclusion (CASE) at the London School of Economics. David Piachaud is Professor of Social Policy at the London School of Economics and an Associate of CASE.

First published 2003 by the Joseph Rowntree Foundation

ISBN 1 85935 151 4 (paperback)
 1 85935 152 2 (pdf: available at www.jrf.org.uk)

A CIP catalogue record for this report is available from the British Library.

Designed by Adkins Design (www.adkinsdesign.co.uk)
Printed by Fretwells Ltd

Further copies of this report, or any other JRF publication, can be obtained either from the JRF website (www.jrf.org.uk/bookshop/) or from our distributor, York Publishing Services Ltd, 64 Hallfield Road, Layerthorpe, York YO31 7ZQ (Tel: 01904 430033).

Contents

■ Acknowledgements

This research was supported by the Joseph Rowntree Foundation, to whom we are grateful; in particular, we would like to thank Barbara Ballard. Data from the Family Resources Survey have been made available by the Department for Work and Pensions (DWP) and data from the Family Expenditure Survey have been made available by the Office for National Statistics (ONS), both through the UK Data Archive. The ONS also kindly provided some of the assumptions used in the chapter on indirect taxes. The DWP, ONS and the Data Archive bear no responsibility for the analysis or interpretation of the data reported here.

We have benefited from expert assistance from Gundi Knies, Lavinia Mitton, Ceema Namazie and Jaime Ruiz-Tagle and received very helpful comments on an earlier draft from Tony Atkinson, Fran Bennett, Jonathan Bradshaw, Charlotte Clark, Donald Hirsch, Caroline Lakin and Abigail McKnight. John Hills, Director of the Centre for Analysis of Social Exclusion, has provided encouragement, support and wise counsel throughout. None of these people should be held responsible for any errors that remain or the opinions expressed in this paper.

1 Introduction ■

How and why has poverty in Britain changed? How is it likely to change as a result of changes in benefits, direct taxes and indirect taxes? These are the questions with which this report is concerned.

The election of a new government in 1997 brought renewed policy concern with poverty and opportunities for all. In the run-up to the 1997 election, the Labour Party had made Britain's growing social inequality a central issue. Since 1979 the proportion of children living in poverty had tripled. The Budgets of 1997 and 1998 emphasised fairness. It was not until 1999, however, that the government set a specific objective concerning poverty. The Prime Minister set the goal of ending child poverty within a generation; the more specific target of halving it by 2010 was stated soon after.

The current Public Service Agreement (PSA) target for reduction in child poverty by one quarter applies to the period 1998/9 to 2004/5. In this study we consider the record of the Labour government since they came to office in May 1997, and look ahead as far as the tax-benefit system applying in 2003/4. We start with the tax-benefit system April 1997, corresponding to the system that the Labour government inherited when it came to power. This pre-dates the child poverty target baseline year. Moreover, there is an additional year after 2003/4 for possible changes – to policies and to incomes generally – before it will be possible to judge whether the target has been met. So our analysis of the impact on poverty of the changes introduced up to 2003/4 is relevant to the general goal of reducing child poverty by one quarter, rather than the specific target.

Estimates made by HM Treasury (2001) and independent research by Piachaud and Sutherland (2001) – both using policy simulation methods – suggested that policy changes would reduce the extent of child poverty by about 1 million by 2002, below what it would otherwise have been. In the event, government estimates of the actual change in child poverty between 1996/7 and 2000/1 only indicated a fall of half a million. Part of the explanation for this apparent discrepancy is that not all the policy changes modelled in the earlier work had actually taken effect by March 2001. However, the discrepancy also serves to highlight the fact that changes in poverty are not only the result of policy changes but also result from other economic and social changes. One of the purposes of this report is to analyse these changes, as well as examining the impact of policy change.[1]

One basic problem in researching policy changes is that evidence of their impact is often only available long after they have taken effect. This is certainly true of evidence on poverty. Even though publication of government poverty estimates in *Households Below Average Income*

(HBAI: Department for Work and Pensions 2003) has been speeded up, the latest published estimates relate to 2001/2.

Another problem in discussing poverty is that few agree on its meaning or measurement. Here, it is generally assumed that poverty should be measured relative to prevailing income levels, but until recently the most commonly used poverty level was 50 per cent of mean disposable income adjusted for household size. More recently European studies have tended to use a standard of 60 per cent of the contemporary median income level adjusted for household size and the British government have used it in their reports on *Opportunity for All* (DWP 2002a). The use of the median rather than mean reduces the impact that changes in the very highest incomes may have on the poverty line. As an indicator of the 'middle' income level, the median is clearly preferable. The poverty level of 60 per cent of the median is close to the level of 50 per cent of the mean and is used in this report.

This report is concerned with poverty as a whole but it is especially focused on child poverty and on pensioners. The focus on child poverty is because it is the only type of poverty for which the government has set a specific goal and because of the mass of evidence that child

Table 1 **Proportion below 60% of median income**			
	All individuals (%)	**Children (%)**	**Pensioners (%)**
Before housing costs (BHC)			
1994/5	18	23	21
1995/6	17	21	22
1996/7	18	25	21
1997/8	18	25	22
1998/9	18	24	23
1999/00	18	23	22
2000/1	17	21	21
2001/2	17	21	22
After housing costs (AHC)			
1994/5	24	32	27
1995/6	23	32	25
1996/7	25	34	27
1997/8	24	33	27
1998/9	24	33	27
1999/00	23	32	25
2000/1	23	31	24
2001/2	22	30	22

Source: Households Below Average Income (DWP 2003).

poverty is important for children's opportunities and thus for future poverty. The focus on pensioners is because this group has been targeted for significant policy changes.

The HBAI estimates of the extent of poverty are shown in Table 1.

The first part of this report analyses the changes that occurred between 1996/7 and 2000/1 and assesses the potential impact of policy changes coming into effect after March 2001. Some of this report draws on existing published evidence. Much, however, draws on original analyses of data from the Family Resources Survey (FRS) for 1996/7 and 2000/1 on which the Households Below Average Income (HBAI) estimates are based. (Although HBAI results for 2001/2 have been published, at the time of writing – March 2003 – the underlying FRS micro-data for 2001/2 are not yet not available.)

The structure of the report is as follows.

Chapter 2 examines the changes in poverty between 1996/7 and 2000/1, and analyses explanations of these changes; it also seeks to resolve the apparent discrepancy between early estimates of the impact of policy changes and what actually happened over time. Our analysis uses the same micro-data, methods and assumptions as that in HBAI, and extends it in various ways.

The possible impact of policy changes made or announced after March 2001 is considered in Chapter 3. This is based on a simulation of their impact on a sample of households from the FRS for 1999/2000. Unlike Chapter 2, which examines what actually changed, Chapter 3 is based on simulations using assumptions about other changes in the economy. Chapter 4 examines the sensitivity of some of the results to the assumptions and methods used.

In addition to the changes in benefits and in direct taxes considered in Chapters 2 and 3, there have also been changes in indirect taxes. Their impact on poverty has not been systematically assessed before. This is done in Chapter 5.

Finally, in Chapter 6, we set out our conclusions.

■ 2 Poverty 1996/7–2000/1

The extent of poverty

Throughout this report poverty is measured on the basis of household disposable income adjusted for household size (or 'equivalised' income). The methods, data and assumptions are described in Appendix I. In line with the Households Below Average Income (HBAI) studies, two measures are used – 'before housing costs' (BHC) and 'after housing costs' (AHC). For each household its equivalised income level (i.e. adjusted for household size) is calculated. This income level is assigned to all members of the household on the assumption that income is shared equally within the household. (While this is the standard assumption, it must be recognised that it is not a valid assumption for many households). In analysing family and economic circumstances this is done on the basis of 'benefit units' which broadly correspond to nuclear families; while most households only comprise one benefit unit, some comprise two or more units. The benefit units are particularly important since policies affecting family benefits and tax credits mostly operate at the benefit unit level.

The poverty lines used here are based on 60 per cent of contemporary median equivalised income. The DWP is currently consulting on the best way of measuring child poverty. Since we do not yet know their final conclusions, we use the number of people below this poverty line as being the poverty indicator around which there has been most consensus both in the UK and in the European Union (although it is often now referred to as indicating 'being at risk of poverty').

The poverty levels for couples without children, expressed in 2000/1 prices, are:

	1996/7	2000/1
BHC	£161	£176
AHC	£136	£153

These levels rose in line with median incomes, in real terms by 9.3 per cent (BHC) and 12.8 per cent (AHC) between 1996/7 and 2000/1.

The extent of poverty by family type in 1996/7 and 2000/1 is shown in Table 2. Overall there was a small reduction in poverty based on income before housing costs (–1.4 per cent) and a slightly bigger fall after housing costs (–2 per cent). This represents an overall fall in the number of individuals in poor households of some 0.8–1.1 million.

Table 2 Extent of poverty by family type

	Proportion poor (%)	
	1996/7	**2000/1**
BHC		
Pensioner couple	19.9	21.9
Single pensioner	23.1	21.4
Couple with children	19.0	15.7
Couple without children	9.7	10.1
Single with children	37.5	32.3
Single without children	16.1	16.3
All households	18.4	17.0
AHC		
Pensioner couple	22.3	21.8
Single pensioner	32.5	28.2
Couple with children	23.0	20.9
Couple without children	11.9	12.2
Single with children	62.0	53.8
Single without children	24.3	21.7
All households	24.6	22.6

Poverty threshold: 60% of median income.
Source: Own calculations from 1996/7 and 2000/1 FRS micro-data using the same methods and assumptions as HBAI statistics.

The highest incidence of poverty was among people in lone-parent families, particularly when measured after housing costs. The biggest falls occurred among families with children whether couples or lone parents.

The extent of child poverty is shown in Table 3. Children in larger two-parent families are twice as likely to be poor as children in smaller families, and those in lone-parent families are even more prone to poverty.

Between 1996/7 and 2000/1 child poverty fell and it did so in all family types and on both measures. The largest falls were in larger and lone-parent families. The extent of the fall differs according to the measure used – 4.2 percentage points or one-sixth on the BHC measure, 3.5 percentage points or one-tenth on the AHC measure. This represents reductions of 540,000 and 450,000 respectively in the number of children in poverty.

Table 3 Extent of child poverty by family composition

	Proportion poor (%)	
	1996/7	**2000/1**
BHC		
Couple: 1 or 2 children	13.3	12.5
Couple: 3 or more children	36.6	26.6
Lone parent: 1 or more children	40.0	34.1
All children	25.5	21.3
AHC		
Couple: 1 or 2 children	17.5	17.0
Couple: 3 or more children	40.0	33.8
Lone parent: 1 or more children	63.9	55.3
All children	34.0	30.5

Source: Own calculations from 1996/7 and 2000/1 FRS micro-data using the same methods and assumptions as HBAI statistics.

Explaining changes in poverty

The purpose of this section is to examine the changes that occurred between 1996/7 and 2000/1 and to assess their possible impact on poverty. Since poverty is not uniform in all groups, the amount of poverty can increase either if a group with a high poverty rate grows in numbers – 'compositional' changes – or if the poverty rate for a particular group rises – 'incidence' changes. The basis for distinguishing 'compositional' changes and 'incidence' changes is set out in Appendix II.

Population changes

Changes in the demographic composition of the population between 1996/7 and 2000/1 are shown in Table 4. In general these changes have been quite small. There were half a million fewer in 'couples with children' and 200,000 more in 'single with children' families. The biggest change was an increase of 1 million single non-pensioners without children. The effects of the compositional changes on poverty were very small, increasing poverty by 0.1 (BHC) and 0.2 (AHC) percentage points. Similarly the impact on child poverty attributable to changes in family composition is very small.

Overall, recent changes in poverty cannot be explained by changes in family type among the population.

Table 4 **Distribution of individuals by family status of benefit unit, 1996/7 and 2000/1**

Family type	Proportion of individuals (%)	
	1996/7	**2000/1**
Pensioner couple	9.4	9.5
Single pensioner	7.5	7.4
Couple with children	36.6	35.3
Couple without children	21.8	21.3
Single with children	8.2	8.4
Single without children	16.5	18.3
Total (numbers in millions)	**56.3m**	**56.9m**

Source: Own calculations from 1996/7 and 2000/1 FRS micro-data using the same methods and assumptions as HBAI statistics.

Changes in employment situation

What was the impact of changes in people's employment situation? The changes that occurred are shown in Tables 5 and 6. There were marked differences between the 1996/7 and 2000/1 samples. Self-employed numbers fell and those in units where all the adult(s) were in a full-time job increased substantially. The number of individuals in units where the head or spouse was unemployed fell by over 1 million from 5.2 per cent to 3.1 per cent. The changes in employment situation account for a considerable change in poverty. Using the before housing cost measure, there was a fall in total poverty attributable to the changing employment situation of 1.3 percentage points (Table 5) and a fall in child poverty of 2.3 percentage points (Table 6). Using the after housing cost measure, the changing employment situation – especially the fall in numbers in unemployed units – accounted for most of the overall fall in poverty both generally and among children.

These figures must be treated with caution for two reasons. First, the data are based on two discrete surveys and does not follow the same individuals between the two years that are compared. Second, the earnings of those formerly unemployed tend to be lower than average (McKnight 2000). Nevertheless, changes in the employment situation appear to have contributed to a fall in total poverty of up to one and a half percentage points, resulting overall in about 800,000 fewer people in poverty including some 300,000 fewer poor children. Between 1996/7 and 2000/1 changes in employment therefore acted to reduce poverty.

Table 5 The effect of the changing composition of the population on the overall poverty rate: Employment situation

	Proportion of population (%)		Proportion poor (%)		Compositional effect[1]	Incidence effect[1]	Combined effect[1]
	1996/7 p97	2000/1 p01	1996/7 p97	2000/1 p01	x	y	z
BHC							
Self-employed	10.1	9.0	18.6	19.3	–0.01	0.07	0.06
Single or couple, all in full-time work	22.5	24.9	1.9	2.5	–0.38	0.15	–0.23
Couple, one in full-time work, one part-time	14.1	14.5	2.7	2.8	–0.06	0.01	–0.04
Couple, one full-time work, one not working	12.2	11.9	15.4	13.5	0.01	–0.23	–0.22
One or more in part-time work	7.4	8.3	25.0	22.3	0.05	–0.21	–0.16
Head or spouse aged 60 or over	17.4	17.2	23.6	24.1	–0.01	0.09	0.07
Head or spouse unemployed	5.2	3.1	61.7	63.6	–0.94	0.08	–0.86
Other	10.9	11.0	42.3	42.1	0.02	–0.02	0.01
All households	**100.0**	**100.0**	**18.4**	**17.0**	**–1.31**	**–0.06**	**–1.37**
AHC							
Self-employed	10.1	9.0	21.9	24.6	0.00	0.26	0.26
Single or couple, all in full-time work	22.5	24.9	3.1	4.0	–0.49	0.22	–0.27
Couple, one in full-time work, one part-time	14.1	14.5	4.4	5.1	–0.07	0.11	0.03
Couple, one full-time work, one not working	12.2	11.9	20.5	19.7	0.01	–0.09	–0.08
One or more in part-time work	7.4	8.3	31.9	29.4	0.06	–0.19	–0.13
Head or spouse aged 60 or over	17.4	17.2	29.8	27.6	–0.01	–0.38	–0.39
Head or spouse unemployed	5.2	3.1	77.8	77.0	–1.12	–0.03	–1.15
Other	10.9	11.0	63.9	60.8	0.04	–0.34	–0.30
All households	**100.0**	**100.0**	**24.6**	**22.6**	**–1.57**	**–0.45**	**–2.02**

Source: Own calculations from 1996/7 and 2000/1 FRS micro-data using the same methods and assumptions as HBAI statistics.
Note: 1 See Appendix II.

Table 6 The effect of the changing composition of the population on the child poverty rate: Employment situation

	Proportion of child population (%)		Proportion poor (%)		Compositional effect[1] x	Incidence effect[1] y	Combined effect[1] z
	1996/7 p97	2000/1 p01	1996/7 p97	2000/1 p01			
BHC							
Self-employed	12.9	11.5	24.1	23.6	-0.01	-0.06	-0.06
Single or couple, all in full-time work	14.2	16.7	2.5	2.1	-0.54	-0.06	-0.60
Couple, one in full-time work, one part-time	21.9	23.4	3.6	3.3	-0.30	-0.08	-0.38
Couple, one in full-time work, one not working	18.2	17.5	21.3	17.9	0.03	-0.60	-0.57
One or more in part-time work	7.8	9.6	38.5	29.9	0.19	-0.74	-0.55
Head or spouse aged 60 or over	0.5	0.6	59.0	62.9	0.04	0.02	0.07
Head or spouse unemployed	6.6	3.6	73.8	71.5	-1.47	-0.12	-1.58
Other	17.9	17.0	51.6	50.0	-0.26	-0.28	-0.54
All households	**100.0**	**100.0**	**25.5**	**21.3**	**-2.31**	**-1.91**	**-4.22**
AHC							
Self-employed	12.9	11.5	28.1	30.8	0.04	0.33	0.37
Single or couple, all in full-time work	14.2	16.7	3.3	4.5	-0.73	0.18	-0.55
Couple, one in full-time work, one part-time	21.9	23.4	5.5	6.2	-0.39	0.14	-0.26
Couple, one full-time work, one not working	18.2	17.5	27.1	25.2	0.04	-0.34	-0.29
One or more in part-time work	7.8	9.6	48.7	42.2	0.23	-0.56	-0.33
Head or spouse aged 60 or over	0.5	0.6	66.2	61.5	0.04	-0.03	0.01
Head or spouse unemployed	6.6	3.6	89.0	90.1	-1.71	0.05	-1.65
Other	17.9	17.0	76.8	74.7	-0.41	-0.36	-0.77
All households	**100.0**	**100.0**	**34.0**	**30.5**	**-2.89**	**-0.58**	**-3.46**

Source: Own calculations from 1996/7 and 2000/1 FRS micro-data using the same methods and assumptions as HBAI statistics.
Note: 1 See Appendix II.

Earnings

Earnings are the single biggest component of income. Lack of earnings has been and remains the major cause of poverty. The level of earnings is crucial to income level. How then have earnings changed?

What matters for poverty is the total earnings received by all members of the income unit. Changes in weekly earnings of full-time workers are shown in Table 7; this compares the changes recorded in the FRS with those in the New Earnings Survey (NES). The picture both surveys give of the change in median earnings and the distribution of earnings – which is crucial for poverty – is almost identical. The average weekly earnings of full-time workers at the lower end, relative to median earnings, changed very little. Whatever the impact of the introduction of the national minimum wage on those with the lowest hourly earnings, it had little apparent impact on reducing inequality of weekly earnings among the full-time working poor (as shown by the figures for the bottom decile and lower quartile compared with the median).

Not all the poor are on low hourly earnings and not all those on low hourly earnings are poor. The distribution of hourly wages in relation to household income level is shown for 2000/1 in Table 8; this relationship had changed very little between 1996/7 and 2000/1.

Table 7 Weekly earnings distribution estimates (full-time workers only)

		1996/7	2000/1	Change 1996/7–2000/1
Median earnings				
(at 2000/1 prices) (£/week)	NES[1]	344	362	+5.2%
	FRS	319	335	+5.0%
Bottom decile as %				
of median	NES[2]	55.7%	55.9%	+0.2%
	FRS	50.0%	51.0%	+1.0%
Lower quartile as %				
of median	NES[2]	72.4%	72.3%	−0.1%
	FRS	69.2%	70.4%	+1.2%

Sources: FRS: Own calculation from 1996/7 and 2000/1 FRS micro-data using the same methods and assumptions as HBAI statistics.
NES: Table A30, *New Earnings Survey*, Office for National Statistics, 2002.

Notes: 1 Mean of NES at beginning and end of year.
2 End year NES.

Table 8 Hourly wages and income levels, 2000/1

	Distribution of income BHC, equivalised as % of median					
	<60	**60–79**	**80–99**	**100–149**	**>150%**	**Total**
Distribution of hourly wage						
< 60% median	16.0	21.5	21.2	29.9	11.4	100.0
	50.2	32.8	22.4	13.0	4.8	15.2
60–79% median	7.6	16.6	21.7	38.3	15.8	100.0
	26.9	28.6	25.8	18.9	7.5	17.1
80–99% median	4.0	10.7	19.4	43.1	22.7	100.0
	13.6	17.6	22.0	20.2	10.3	16.3
100–149% median	1.4	6.3	11.8	39.8	40.7	100.0
	7.9	17.1	22.2	31.1	30.6	27.1
>150% of median	0.3	1.6	4.5	24.0	69.6	100.0
	1.4	3.9	7.6	16.8	46.9	24.3
Total	**4.8**	**10.0**	**14.4**	**34.8**	**36.1**	**100.0**
	100.0	**100.0**	**100.0**	**100.0**	**100.0**	**100.0**

Source: Own calculations from 1996/7 and 2000/1 FRS micro-data using the same methods and assumptions as HBAI statistics.

Benefits and taxes

Most of those on low incomes are dependent in whole or in part on incomes from the state. Indeed, social security originated as a mechanism for achieving freedom from want. The social security system has been reformed since 1997, not least in terminology and organisation. The Department of Social Security has been replaced by the Department for Work and Pensions; responsibility for National Insurance contributions and for the main elements of the financial support for children has been transferred to the Inland Revenue; and much of the administration has been devolved to specialised agencies. Because of the complex changes it is all the more important – if more difficult – to assess the impact of these changes in benefits and taxes. In this chapter only changes in benefits and direct taxes are considered; changes in indirect taxes are considered in Chapter 5.

The real values of the principal social security benefits are set out in Table 9. This is based on DWP calculations using the average value of the retail price index between upratings. It will be seen that comparing 1996/7 and 2000/1 some of the benefits were worth less in real terms but there were differences in the extent of the fall. (Some small differences are due to

Table 9 Values of social security benefits (at April 2001 prices, £ per week)

	1996/7	2000/1	Change (%)
Basic retirement pension			
Single	68.86	68.21	−0.9
Couple	110.07	109.03	−0.9
Jobseekers allowance (contributory)			
Single	54.33	52.75	−2.9
Couple	87.09	82.81	−4.9
Incapacity benefit (long term single)	68.86	68.21	−0.9
Child benefit			
1st child	12.16	15.16	+24.7
2nd + child	9.91	10.11	+2.0
Income support			
Single 18–24	41.30	41.75	+1.1
Single over 25	53.95	52.71	−2.3
Couple, no child	84.70	82.75	−2.3
Couple, 1 child (under 11)	111.36	124.00	+9.2
Couple, 2 children (under 11)	129.28	150.86	+16.7
Lone parent, 1 child (under 11)	87.28	93.76	+7.4

Source: Section 5, *Abstract of Statistics* (DWP, 2001 edition).

uprating being based on a lagged price adjustment.) Apart from the benefits specifically for children, all of the main benefits fell relative to median incomes (which rose in real terms by 10 per cent (BHC) and 12.5 per cent (AHC)).

The Department for Work and Pensions also calculates the notional value of all benefits and tax credits for model families at different earning levels. The effects of changes in these between April 1996 and April 2000 on net incomes are shown in Table 10. Net incomes for notional single people and childless couples on low or average earnings rose at broadly the same rate as median incomes. For notional families with children with an adult on low earnings, the combination of changes in earnings, benefits and tax credits resulted in substantial increases in net incomes.

The rates of minimum income provided by Income Support are substantially below the poverty level. This is especially true for families with children, as shown in Table 11.

The impact of changes
The combined impact of all the changes may be represented diagrammatically as is done with distributions of income in Figure 1 for all individuals and Figure 2 for children. The

Table 10 **Real increase in net income after housing costs (April 1996–April 2000, £ per week)**

	Single	Couple 0 child	Couple 1 child	Couple 2 children	Single parent 1 child
Average earnings	10.8	8.3	8.9	9.2	7.8
2/3 average earnings	11.5	7.6	13.1	26.6	20.8
1/2 average earnings	12.2	6.8	25.2	29.0	13.5

Source: Section 4, *Abstract of Statistics* (DWP, 2001 edition).

Notes: Net income is defined as earnings: less income tax, less National Insurance contributions, less rent and local taxes, plus benefits and housing benefit, plus Inland Revenue tax credits. Net incomes are converted to April 2001 price levels.

Table 11 **Income support levels as % of poverty level (60% of median AHC) 2000/1**

	Poverty level (£/week)	Income Support (£/week)	IS as % of poverty level
Couple, 1 child (aged 8)	188.20	125.00	66.4
Couple, 2 children (aged 8, 11)	228.00	153.80	67.4
Couple, 3 children (aged 3, 8, 11)	255.60	182.50	71.4
1 adult, 1 child (aged 8)	119.30	81.00	67.9

cumulative frequency distributions for children only are shown in Figure 3. These show a small overall shift from just below to just above the poverty line. The pattern is similar for all individuals and children although with larger reductions in the case of children.

Few children in inactive and unemployed families have moved across the poverty line, though there is some evidence that unemployed families have moved nearer the poverty line. There is also evidence that some more inactive units are worse off than in 1996/7 and that the distribution of incomes within this group is more spread out.

Children in families with part-time workers seemed to have benefited most over this period with quite a significant shift from below to above the relative poverty line, although these account for less than one-tenth of all children. For children in families with one full-time worker and one non-worker, there is a very slight reduction in the relative poverty rate. For children in other economically active units, there is evidence that the peaks in the distributions have shifted to the left (i.e. nearer the relative poverty line), although this has only led to a very slight increase in the relative poverty rate for these groups because most of the movement is taking place above the poverty line. There was little change in the relative poverty rate for children in self-employed families.

Figure 1 Distribution of incomes – all individuals

(a) BHC

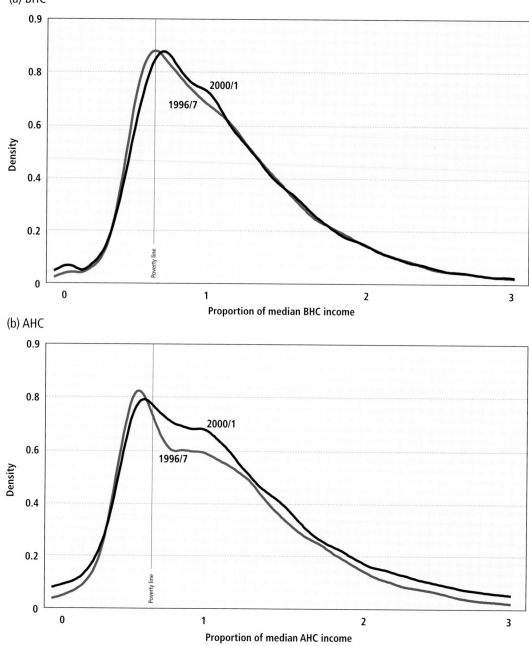

Proportion of median BHC income

(b) AHC

Proportion of median AHC income

Figure 2 Distribution of incomes – children

(a) BHC

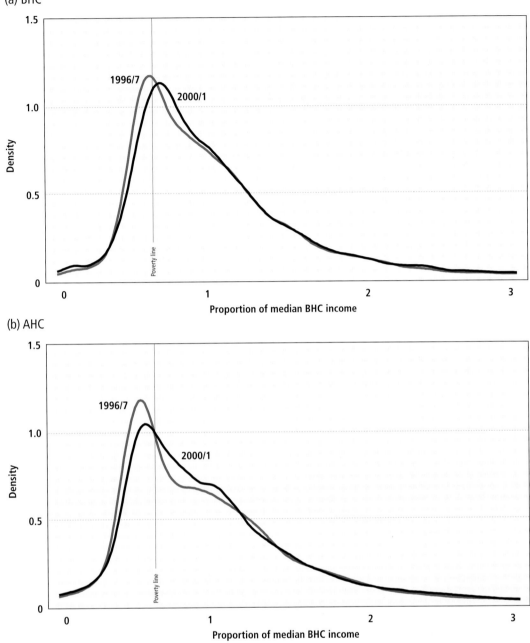

(b) AHC

Figure 3 **Percentage of children in households with incomes below proportions of the median: 1996/7 and 2000/1**

(a) BHC

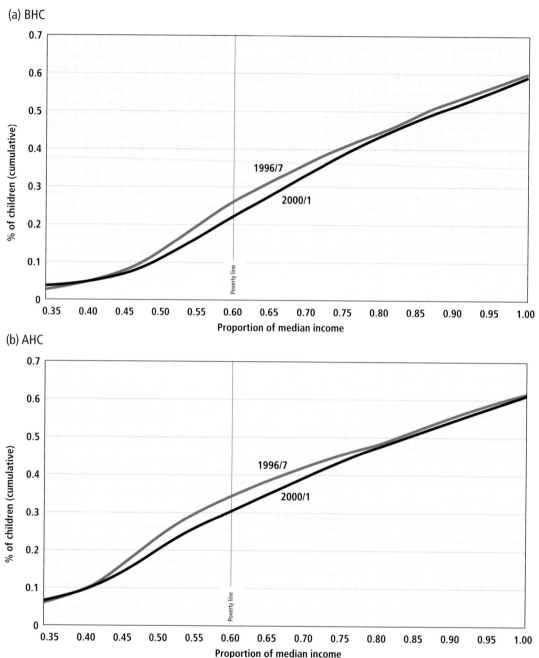

Overall explanations of changes in poverty

The purpose of Chapter 2 has been to consider the changes in relative poverty between 1996/7 and 2000/1 and why they occurred.

A note of caution is necessary. We do not know the actual changes in numbers of those in poverty. All we know are the estimates based on the FRS. While these are the best available estimates, they are subject to error from a number of sources (see Appendix II of DWP (2002)). An important source of error which can be quantified is sampling error. Using

95 per cent confidence intervals, the possible numbers in poverty (assuming sampling errors in 1996/7 were similar to those in 2000/1) were:

		All poverty	Child poverty
BHC	1996/7	10.0–10.8m	3.2–3.5m
	2000/1	9.3–10.1m	2.6–2.9m
AHC	1996/7	13.5–14.3m	4.3–4.6m
	2000/1	12.5–13.3m	3.8–4.1m

Source: DWP (2002) Appendix Table 2.4

Thus while the central HBAI estimate is that total poverty fell by 700,000 (BHC) and 1.0 million (AHC), the change could lie between a rise of 100,000 and a fall of 1.5 million (BHC) and a fall of between 200,000 and 1.8 million (AHC). The fall in child poverty could lie between 300,000 and 900,000 (BHC) and between 200,000 and 800,000 (AHC). What does seem certain is that child poverty fell between 1996/7 and 2000/1, but by how much cannot be known with certainty.

As discussed in the introduction to this report, much attention has been focused on the contrast between estimates of the modelled impact effects of policy changes on child poverty and the central estimate of the actual changes that occurred. Why, if the former suggested a fall of about 1 million, did child poverty only fall by half a million? The apparent discrepancy seems all the worse since the fall in unemployment tended to reduce child poverty so that the number might have been expected to fall by more than 1 million.

There are two principal explanations for the apparent discrepancy.

The first, relatively straightforward, explanation is that estimates of the effects of policy changes included measures taking effect in 2001/2 (that is, after the 2000/1 period on which the latest results reported above are based). These included, among other things, the introduction of the Children's Tax Credit, an extension of the 10p band of income tax, and increases in means-tested benefits for pensioners. Therefore we would not expect 2000/1 poverty estimates to match simulation results for the following year's policies.

The major explanation for the apparent discrepancy is that Treasury and our own estimates of the effect of policy changes were just that – estimates of the effects of policy changes taken by themselves. They aimed to answer the question 'How did the new policy affect the number in poverty compared to the old policy?' Actual changes in poverty depend both on changes in the incomes of those close to the poverty line and, crucially, on the changes in median incomes which determine the change in the level of the poverty line. If the poverty line rises over time in real terms, part of the 'impact' effect of policy changes is needed simply for the relative poverty rate to stand still.

This inter-relationship makes understanding actual changes in poverty somewhat difficult.

If all earnings and incomes changed by the same amount, if benefits rose at the same rate, and there were no changes in the way people organise themselves into households, then there would be no change in poverty.

Many changes could reduce poverty. There would be a fall:

- if rich and poor people decided to live together
- if earnings for the low paid increased
- if people moved from relatively low incomes on social security benefits into employment on higher earned incomes
- if benefits and pensions improved relative to median incomes.

In this study, along with much other analysis (and the government's own short-term targets), it has been assumed that the poverty line should rise at the same rate as median income levels. Clearly if the poverty level is kept fixed in real terms then the reduction in poverty would be much greater. For instance, instead of a 1.4 (BHC) or 2.0 (AHC) percentage point reduction in the proportion in poverty, using the 1996/7 constant real poverty level there would have been a fall of 5 (BHC) or 8 (AHC) percentage points, or 4.1 or 3.1 million people respectively, by 2000/1.

The overall explanation for the changes in relative poverty that occurred between 1996/7 and 2000/1 is fairly clear. The relative poverty line rose by about one-tenth in real terms. There was little change in family types or in the shape of the distribution of earnings. Two things did change. First, unemployment fell and more households had someone in paid employment. Second, policy on benefits and tax credits clearly disadvantaged some and helped others. Those with benefits falling relative to incomes generally were more likely to be losers. They included those on the basic state pension, jobseeker's allowance and incapacity benefit and those on Income Support who did not have children. (In addition lone parent benefits were abolished.) Those more likely to gain were those with children, particularly low earners in employment, and this was a major factor in the reduction by some half a million in the number of children in poverty.

3 Simulating the effects of policy and income changes 1997–2003/4

Simulating changes

So far we have considered the changes in poverty up to March 2001, based on data covering the period April 1996 to March 2001. We can use policy simulation to estimate the effect of changes that took place after this date and also to focus on the effects of policy changes over the whole period 1997–2003/4. More details of the simulation model, POLIMOD, are provided in Appendix III.

Simulating the effects of policy changes on poverty is somewhat complex and it may be helpful to clarify what is involved.

At the simplest level, if we want to assess the impact of specific policy changes at a point in time we can, using a sample of the population at a given time, simulate the effect of changing tax/benefit policy on their incomes. If we wish to estimate the effect of this on poverty (defined as below 60 per cent of current median income) then we must make an adjustment in the poverty line depending on the effect of the policy changes on median income.

To simulate the impact of policy changes over a number of years there are two possible approaches:

(a) Assuming constant incomes
To assess the effect of policy changes alone we can convert the policies in different years to a constant price basis and apply policies for different years to a sample with constant incomes.

To look at the effects on poverty we must make an adjustment in the poverty line depending on the effect of the policy changes on median income. This approach is adopted in the section considering the effects of policy changes alone (page 26). Household disposable incomes are re-calculated according to the policies that prevailed in 1997 and 2000/1 and policies announced for 2003/4. Policies are re-based in 2000/1 prices.

(b) Assuming changing incomes
In practice, incomes change over time. The main reason in the period under review has been the rise in earnings but other income components have changed by different amounts. Changing incomes result in different taxes and benefits and in changes in median incomes and in the level of the poverty line.

The rise in the value of different income components can be estimated from aggregate data and used to construct datasets containing adjusted pre-tax and benefit incomes, one for each year under consideration (assuming fixed composition in terms of household sizes, employment etc.). The tax/benefit policies for the relevant years can then be applied to the simulated dataset for that year. The level of the poverty line changes in part because of the effect of the tax/benefit changes and in part because of the income changes. For comparability between years, all income data can be converted to a constant price basis.

This approach is adopted below in the section 'Changes in poverty: 1997, 2000/1 and 2003/4 policies and incomes' (page 30). Policy changes are simulated as in the section 'The effects of policy changes alone'. In addition, pre-tax and benefit incomes (earnings, occupational pensions, income from investments etc.) and housing costs (mortgage interest, rent) are backdated to 1997 real levels and projected to 2003/4 real levels, in 2000/1 prices.

In theory it would also be possible to examine the interacting effects of the changing composition of the population (i.e. changes in family composition, changes in employment and unemployment etc.). However, it would be very difficult to capture all of the relevant interacting changes in order to estimate accurately, for example, the number of lone parents in paid work, or to predict changes up to 2003/4.

The policy simulations that are presented here are based on data derived from the Family Resources Survey 1999/2000. The changes in tax and benefit policy that are simulated are set out in Appendix IV. The method of updating the FRS data to 2000/1 is set out in Appendix V.

Policy simulation estimates allow us to focus on the direct effects of policy. The section 'The effects of policy changes alone' (below) considers the direct effects of policy changes – the components of the changing picture that are under direct government control. The section 'Changes in poverty' (page 30) focuses on the combined effect of policy changes and rising incomes, allowing us to explore the size and nature of the effect of rising real incomes and an upward shifting poverty line on poverty estimates. Two sub-sections focus on children and pensioners respectively (pages 30 and 35). The partial picture provided by the simulation estimates presented in this chapter naturally differs from the 'full' actual or outcome picture provided in Chapter 2. The differences and the reasons for the differences are then discussed ('The relationship between policy simulation results and HBAI statistics') and the final section summarises the main findings of the chapter.

The effects of policy changes alone

In order to examine the impact of policy changes on poverty, the most appropriate method is that outlined in the section 'Assuming constant incomes' (page 25). This focuses on changes in poverty caused by policy changes without considering changes in poverty due to other changes in income levels. It does, however, adjust the poverty line for changes in median income that result directly from the policy changes.

In this section therefore we examine the impact of the direct policy changes alone, without also trying to capture the – mainly exogenous – real changes in pre-tax benefit incomes. We adjust the parameters of the 1997 and 2003/4 tax-benefit systems to 2000/1 prices and explore the effects of these systems on 2000/1 incomes. Appendix IV lists the policy changes that are modelled.

The effects of the three policy regimes on poverty rates using 2000/1 incomes are summarised in Table 12. The impact on the income distribution in relation to the poverty line

Figure 4 **Cumulative proportions of *children* by levels of income, under the policy regimes of 1997, 2000/1 and 2003/4: *constant* (2000/1) incomes**

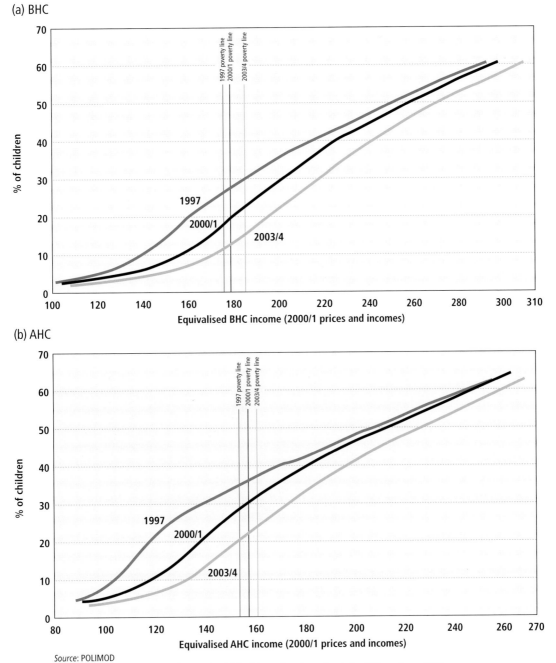

(a) BHC

(b) AHC

Source: POLIMOD

Notes: The distributions are shown from 35% to 100% of the median; observations below 35% are shown at 35%.

under each policy regime is shown in Figures 4 for children and 5 for pensioners. Using this constant income basis, the reduction in child poverty is over 1.3 million or 10 percentage points.[2] On a BHC basis this represents a proportional reduction in child poverty of 41 per cent and on an AHC basis it is a reduction of 30 per cent. If there were no exogenous income growth, as well as no adverse changes in composition such as decreases in employment, the target reduction of 25 per cent would easily be achieved.

Table 12 also shows results for pensioners. In spite of no target reduction for pensioner

Figure 5 **Cumulative proportions of** *people over pension age* **by levels of income, under the policy regimes of 1997, 2000/1 and 2003/4:** *constant* **(2000/1) incomes**

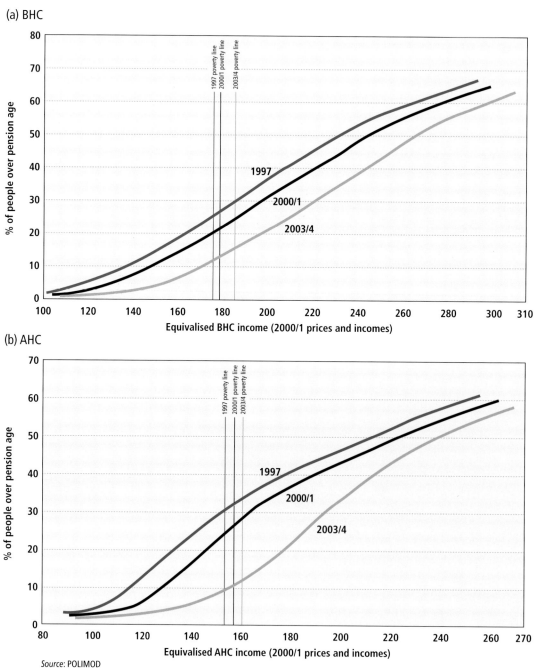

(a) BHC

(b) AHC

Source: POLIMOD

Notes: The distributions are shown from 35% to 100% of the median; observations below 35% are shown at 35%.

Table 12 **Policy simulation estimates of poverty under policy regimes of 1997, 2000/1 and 2003/4, using 2000/1 prices and incomes**

	All		Children		Children in 2 parent families		Children in 1 parent families		People over pension age	
	Number (000)	Rate (%)	Number (000)	Rate (%)	Number (000)	Rate (%)	Number (000)	Rate (%)	Number (000)	Rate (%)
(1) BHC 1997 regime	10,930	19	3,300	26	1,990	20	1,310	43	2,530	25
(2) BHC 2000/1 regime	9,020	16	2,420	19	1,530	16	890	29	2,160	21
(3) BHC 2003/4 regime	7,500	13	1,960	15	1,290	13	660	22	1,550	15
Reduction (1)–(2)	1,910	3	890	7	460	5	420	14	370	4
Reduction (2)–(3)	1,520	3	460	4	240	2	220	7	610	6
Reduction (1)–(3)	3,430	6	1,340	10	700	7	640	21	980	10
(1) AHC 1997 regime	14,160	25	4,420	34	2,440	25	2,000	66	3,050	30
(2) AHC 2000/1 regime	12,910	23	3,870	30	2,200	22	1,670	55	2,640	26
(3) AHC 2003/4 regime	9,800	17	3,080	24	1,770	18	1,320	43	1,210	12
Reduction (1)–(2)	1,250	2	550	4	240	2	330	11	400	4
Reduction (2)–(3)	3,110	5	790	6	430	4	350	12	1,440	14
Reduction (1)–(3)	4,360	8	1,330	10	670	7	680	22	1,840	18

Source: POLIMOD based on 1999/2000 Family Resources Survey data.

Note: Poverty is measured as the numbers of people living in households with equivalised income below 60% of the within-scenario median. Figures are rounded to the nearest 10,000 persons or percentage point. This does not necessarily mean that estimates are statistically significant to the level shown. Rows or columns may not add due to rounding.

poverty the reduction shown on a BHC basis is the same as for children: 10 percentage points, corresponding to nearly 1 million pensioners taken out of poverty. On an AHC basis the reduction is even larger: 18 percentage points or a proportional reduction of more than a half.

Changes in poverty: 1997, 2000/1 and 2003/4 policies and incomes

The changes in poverty based on the current income estimates are shown in Table 13. Here, incomes (earnings, occupation pensions, income from investments, etc.) and housing costs (mortgage interest, rent) are backdated to 1997 real levels and projected to 2003/4 real levels, in 2000/1 prices. Appendix V documents the sources and methods that are used in this updating process.

Overall, the simulation shows a fall in poverty of 1.9 million (BHC) and 3 million (AHC) between 1997 and 2003/4. The two income measures show similar reductions in child poverty over the period (but different results in the sub-periods). The fall in pensioner poverty is much higher on the AHC measure than on the BHC measure.

We first consider child poverty changes, particularly in relation to the target reduction. No such target has been set for pensioner poverty but below we examine the evidence for this group (page 35). These estimates are then compared with actual changes, as measured for 1996/7 to 2000/1 in HBAI.

Child poverty

Using policy simulation estimates shown in Table 13 we can see that child poverty on both a BHC and AHC basis is estimated to be 8 percentage points lower under 2003/4 policies and incomes than under 1997 policies and incomes. These calculations include the direct effects of changes in taxes and benefits and the national minimum wage and the effects of growth in pre-tax and benefit incomes over the period.[3] This reduction represents just over a million fewer children in poverty. The proportional reduction is 33 per cent on a BHC basis and 24 per cent on an AHC basis. Thus – other things being equal – the 2004/5 target for reduction by one-quarter on an AHC basis could be met with a combination of indexing benefit incomes to keep pace with average income growth over the year plus some modest further policy initiatives in 2004. If the target was measured in terms of BHC incomes it appears that it would already be more than met under 2003/4 policies.[4] We return to the question of what is meant by 'other things being equal' in Chapter 4.

Whether or not a child crosses the poverty line depends on two things: how much their own household income increases and how much median incomes increase, pushing up the poverty line. Figure 6 shows both these effects. The position of children is shown according to their household income under the three policy scenarios, and also the corresponding poverty lines (60 per cent of current median income), with all figures expressed in 2000/1 prices. The distributions are shown between 35 per cent and 100 per cent of the median (with those below 35 per cent shown at 35 per cent). We can see that while the income distributions shift to the right, so do the poverty lines, particularly with incomes measured on an AHC

Table 13 Policy simulation estimates of poverty under policy regimes of 1997, 2000/1 and 2003/4, using current prices and incomes

	All		Children		Children in 2 parent families		Children in 1 parent families		People over pension age	
	Number (000)	Rate (%)	Number (000)	Rate (%)	Number (000)	Rate (%)	Number (000)	Rate (%)	Number (000)	Rate (%)
(1) BHC 1997 regime	10,030	18	3,110	24	1,930	20	1,190	39	2,100	21
(2) BHC 2000/1 regime	9,020	16	2,420	19	1,530	16	890	29	2,160	21
(3) BHC 2003/4 regime	8,140	14	2,080	16	1,320	13	770	25	1,830	18
Reduction (1)–(2)	1,010	2	700	5	400	4	300	10	–60	–1
Reduction (2)–(3)	880	2	330	3	210	2	120	4	330	3
Reduction (1)–(3)	1,890	3	1,030	8	610	6	420	14	270	3
(1) AHC 1997 regime	13,530	24	4,290	33	2,380	24	1,900	62	2,710	27
(2) AHC 2000/1 regime	12,910	23	3,870	30	2,200	22	1,670	55	2,640	26
(3) AHC 2003/4 regime	10,560	19	3,250	25	1,790	18	1,460	48	1,500	15
Reduction (1)–(2)	620	1	420	3	190	2	240	8	70	1
Reduction (2)–(3)	2,350	4	620	5	410	4	210	7	1,150	11
Reduction (1)–(3)	2,970	5	1,040	8	590	6	450	15	1,220	12

Source: POLIMOD based on 1999/2000 Family Resources Survey data.

Note: Poverty is measured as the numbers of people living in households with equivalised income below 60% of the within-scenario median. Figures are rounded to the nearest 10,000 persons or percentage point. This does not necessarily mean that estimates are statistically significant to the level shown. Rows or columns may not add due to rounding.

Figure 6 **Proportions of *children* by levels of income, under the policy regimes of 1997, 2000/1 and 2003/4: *current* real incomes**

(a) BHC

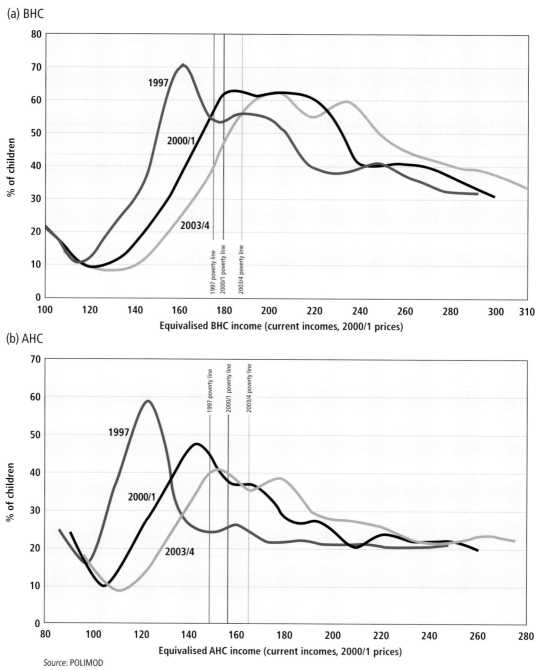

Equivalised BHC income (current incomes, 2000/1 prices)

(b) AHC

Equivalised AHC income (current incomes, 2000/1 prices)

Source: POLIMOD

Notes: The distributions are shown from 35% to 100% of the median; observations below 35% are shown at 35%.

basis. As we have seen, the net effect is a reduction in child poverty but this is much less of a reduction than would be registered if the poverty line were to remain fixed at its 1997 level. The distribution also flattens, which further contributes to poverty reduction, again, particularly with incomes measured on an AHC basis. Generally, it seems that it is the shift of the distribution to the right (net of the shift in poverty line) that has the most effect on a BHC basis and that the flattening of the distribution (the result of policies targeted on poor households with children) has the most effect on an AHC basis.

Figure 7 presents the same information but draws the child income distributions on a cumulative basis. If the poverty line were fixed at its real 1997 level, instead of falling from 33 per cent to 25 per cent, the child poverty rate using AHC incomes would fall to 18 per cent. The figure also demonstrates that the policy changes in the first half of the period (1997–2000/1) tended to have most effect in moving children from well below the poverty line up to it. Changes in the second half of the period tended to benefit children across the whole section of the distribution shown. Table 13 distinguishes children by whether they are living with one parent or two. Child poverty in one-parent families is much higher under the 1997 regime (39 per cent BHC; 62 per cent AHC) compared with the rate in two-parent families (20 per cent BHC; 24 per cent

Figure 7 Cumulative proportions of *children* by levels of income, under the policy regimes of 1997, 2000/1 and 2003/4: *current* real incomes

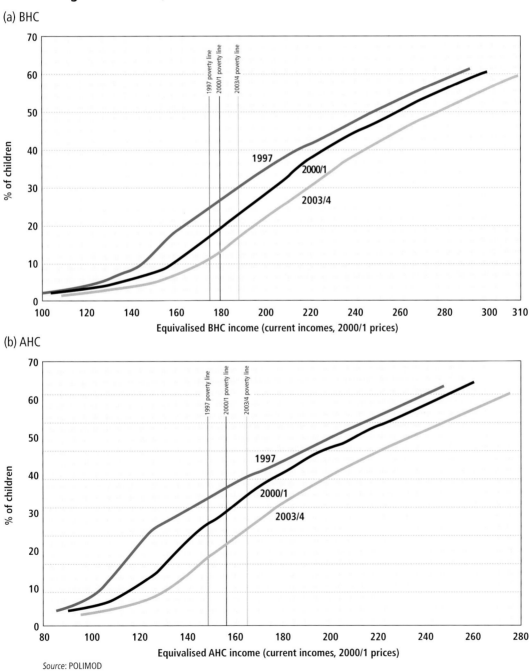

(a) BHC

(b) AHC

Source: POLIMOD
Notes: The distributions are shown from 35% to 100% of the median; observations below 35% are shown at 35%.

AHC). The proportional reduction in child poverty is quite similar in both groups, leaving children in one-parent families with a persistently higher risk of poverty. Using AHC incomes under the 2003/4 regime the rate is 48 per cent, compared with 18 per cent for children in two-parent families. On a BHC basis the poverty rates are 25 per cent and 13 per cent respectively. Figure 8(a) shows the position of children in one-parent families according to their AHC household income in the same way as it is shown for all children in Figure 6(b). It is clear that the distribution of lone-parent incomes is very concentrated around income levels corresponding to Income Support. The degree of concentration becomes less following

Figure 8 **Proportions of *children in one-parent families* by levels of AHC income, under the policy regimes of 1997, 2000/1 and 2003/4**

(a) *Current* real incomes

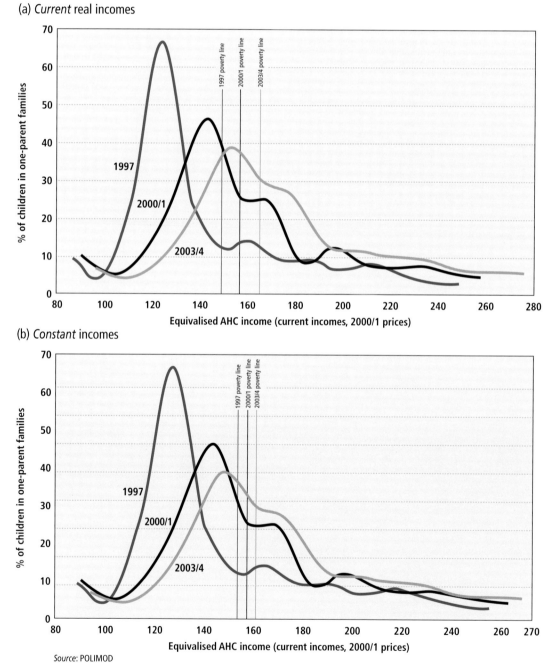

(b) *Constant* incomes

Source: POLIMOD

Notes: The distributions are shown from 35% to 100% of the median; observations below 35% are shown at 35%.

the policy reforms between 1997 and 2003/4. However, the mode of the distribution of children in one-parent families remains persistently below the poverty line even though the gap between mode and poverty line is narrowing. Aside from the income changes considered here we might expect increases in lone-parent employment to have an additional effect in reducing the concentration of lone-parent incomes.

Interestingly, the impact of policy changes on child poverty reduction is substantially lower among children in one-parent families if market incomes are calculated on a current basis than if we assume constant real incomes. This is much less clearly the case for children in two-parent families. The proportional reduction in AHC poverty for children with one parent is 23 per cent compared to 25 per cent for children in two-parent families using current incomes. The corresponding figures assuming constant incomes (Table 12) are 34 per cent and 27 per cent. There are two possible explanations for the differential effects. First, it may be that low income one-parent families are less likely than low income two-parent families to have sources of household income other than benefits. Indeed, earnings make up an average of only 11 per cent of the household incomes of children in lone-parent families counted as poor on an AHC basis under the 2000/1 tax-benefit system. The corresponding figure for children in two-parent families is 45 per cent. This means that low income lone parents are less likely themselves to benefit from real growth in (say) earnings. This is related to the second explanation: we have already seen that there is a concentration of children in one-parent families at a particular level of equivalised AHC income. Poverty rates will be very sensitive to which side of the poverty line this group lies. Figure 8(a) shows that the mode of the 2003/4 distribution remains below the poverty line when this is set in terms of current incomes. Figure 8(b) shows the distribution and the poverty lines using constant incomes on an AHC basis. While Figure 8(a) showed the case where real incomes change (as in Table 13), Figure 8(b) shows the effect of policy changes alone (as in Table 12). The distributions for each of the three policy years are in fact rather similar whether or not pre-tax and benefit incomes are assumed to grow. This is consistent with the receipt of significant amounts of these incomes being atypical among low income one-parent families. Most of the difference in poverty reduction seems to be explained by the difference in the relative positions of the poverty lines in Figure 8 (a) and (b) rather than any difference in lone-parent incomes.

Pensioner poverty

Table 13 shows results for pensioners (defined as women aged 60+ and men aged 65+).[5] First, it is clear that the changes in the first half of the period did little to reduce poverty among pensioners. Indeed, the poverty rate on a BHC basis actually rose by 1 percentage point while the AHC rate fell by only 1 percentage point. In spite of some positive changes in benefits such as the introduction of the winter fuel payment, the policy changes 1997–2000/1 were not sufficient to make up for the upward movement in the poverty line. The policy changes in the second half of the period were more positive and dramatic (including a significant increase in the basic state pension, more substantial increases in means-tested benefits for pensioners – particularly younger pensioners – and the introduction of the Pension Credit in October 2003).[6] This resulted in a poverty rate reduction of 3 percentage points from 21 per cent to 18 per cent between the policy regimes of 2000/1 and 2003/4 on a BHC basis. The reduction on an AHC basis is much bigger – 11 percentage points from 26 per cent to 15 per cent.

This big difference in poverty rate reduction according to the income measure can be understood by looking at a broader picture of the pensioner income distribution in relation to the poverty line. Figure 9 shows the position of pensioners according to their household income under the three policy scenarios. AHC incomes for pensioners are particularly concentrated around one income level (or, under the 2000/1 regime, two levels). The effect is

Figure 9 **Proportions of *people over pension age* by levels of income, under the policy regimes of 1997, 2000/1 and 2003/4: *current* real incomes**

(a) BHC

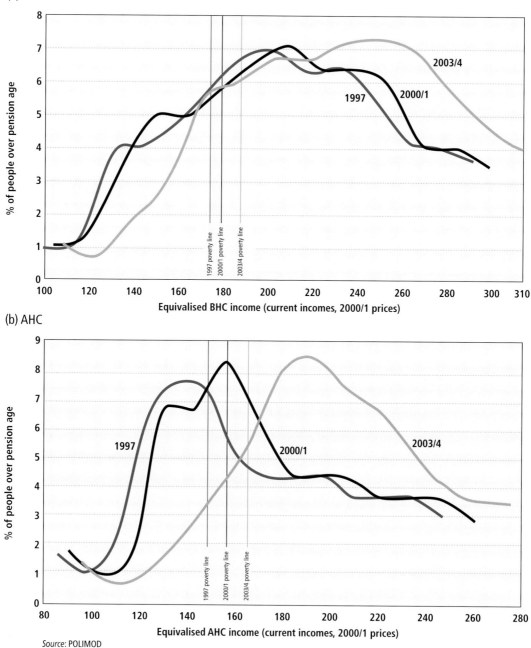

(b) AHC

Source: POLIMOD

Notes: The distributions are shown from 35% to 100% of the median; observations below 35% are shown at 35%.

not quite as marked as for children of lone parents shown in Figure 8, but the explanation is the same. Many low income pensioners are living on identical levels of AHC income – those provided by Income Support (Minimum Income Guarantee (IS/MIG)). On an equivalised basis, benefit incomes for couples are slightly different than those for single pensioners – hence the bi-modal distribution in 2000/1. If the poverty line had remained fixed at its 1997 level in 2000/1, one of the modal parts of the distribution would have risen above the line and pensioner poverty would have appeared to fall further than it did on a relative basis. Using contemporary poverty lines few of the pensioners with household incomes reliant on IS/MIG are taken out of poverty. Under the 2003/4 system, however, minimum incomes for pensioners are increased by enough to move many of them across the poverty line, in spite of significant upward shift in the line.

On a BHC basis there is no single level of income on which large groups of pensioners live. This is because many pensioners on IS/MIG also receive Housing Benefit. The amount of this depends on rent as well as income. Both BHC and AHC incomes include Housing Benefit, but rent is also deducted in the AHC case – exactly neutralising the effect of HB in cases where IS/MIG is received. For this reason the distribution is less 'lumpy' and the numbers of pensioners crossing the poverty line less dramatic.

Both the BHC and AHC versions of Figure 9 indicate a significant improvement in real pensioner incomes under the 2003/4 regime compared with that of 2000/1, and a less clear-cut picture – at least on a BHC basis – for the earlier period. This is more easily seen in Figure 10, which presents the same information but draws the pensioner income distributions on a cumulative basis. The lack of relative improvement in pensioner incomes in the first part of the period is obvious across this whole section of the BHC income distribution. This conclusion about lack of poverty reduction is not at all sensitive to the proportion of median incomes that is defined as the poverty line. On an AHC basis there does appear to have been some improvement but again this applies across the whole of the lower half of the income distribution, as shown. In the second part of the period there is a clear increase in income, particularly on an AHC basis, and targeted on the bottom of the distribution.

The difference shown by using the two income measures is interesting. The difference between BHC and AHC incomes for pensioners tends to be smaller than for the population as a whole, mainly because pensioner owner-occupiers have small or zero debt on which to pay interest.[7] Between 1997 and 2000/1 housing costs rose faster than BHC incomes for the population as a whole, resulting in AHC incomes that grew more slowly than BHC incomes. Generally, pensioner incomes were falling behind those of the rest of the population, so the increase on a BHC basis is small. On an AHC basis it is larger because pensioner housing costs are a smaller component of AHC incomes for this group.

In the second part of the period housing costs grow on average at about the same rate as incomes generally.[8] On both income measures pensioner poverty falls, mainly due to the direct policy changes introduced after March 2001.

Figure 10 Cumulative proportions of *people over pension age* by level of income, under the policy regimes of 1997, 2000/1 and 2003/4: *current* real incomes in 2000/1 prices

(a) BHC

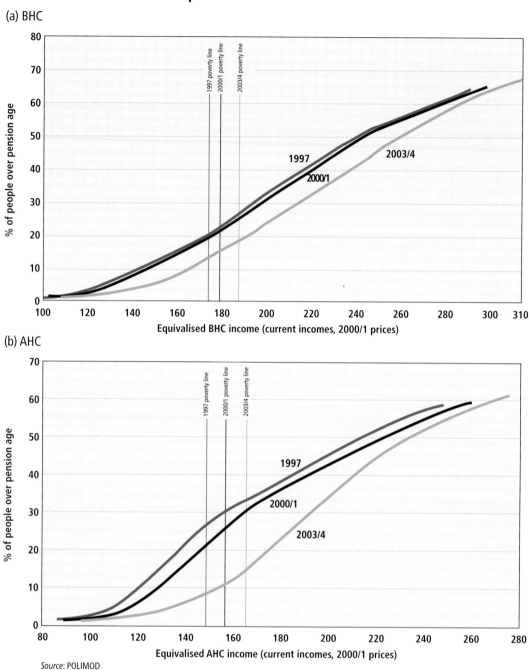

(b) AHC

Source: POLIMOD

Notes: The distributions are shown from 35% to 100% of the median; observations below 35% are shown at 35%.

The relationship between policy simulation results and HBAI statistics

The information in Table 13 allows us to assess the extent to which policy simulation results match reality as captured by statistics taken directly from contemporary survey data. This table shows poverty rates for the whole population and for children using the same definitions of income and poverty as in Chapter 2. It compares these under 1997 policies and incomes with those using 2000/1 policies and incomes. On a BHC basis HBAI statistics show poverty rates falling from 18 per cent to 17 per cent and child poverty rates falling from

26 per cent to 21 per cent (see Table 3) between 1996/7 and 2000/1. POLIMOD estimates show a slightly larger drop in the overall poverty rate (from 18 per cent to 16 per cent) and the same drop in child poverty but from a lower level (5 percentage points from 24 per cent to 19 per cent).

On an AHC basis the fall in the overall rate of poverty is, in contrast, somewhat lower using policy simulation (1 percentage point from 24 per cent to 23 per cent) than in HBAI (2 percentage points from 25 per cent to 23 per cent). It again shows the same drop in child poverty using both methods (3 percentage points), again from a slightly lower starting level with policy simulation compared with HBAI (33 per cent rather than 34 per cent).

Generally these differences look small and may be reassuring in terms of the use of policy simulation to predict changes in poverty rates. However, we found in Chapter 2 that one of the main contributors to the fall in child poverty between 1996/7 and 2000/1 was not policy change but an increase in employment – something not captured by the POLIMOD results in Table 13. If this were the only difference then we would expect policy simulation to underestimate the poverty reduction in fact achieved. There are a number of explanations for why this does not happen.

Some of these result from the assumptions made in the simulation process.[9]

First, we do not simulate the exact policy regime as it existed in 1996/7. Instead we model the system that Labour inherited when it came to power in May 1997, which included the changes introduced by the previous government in April 1997. There were few relevant real changes, except the reduction in the standard rate of income tax from 24 per cent to 23 per cent. This would be likely to increase poverty rates in April 1997 compared with 1996/7 (because of the resulting upward shift in median incomes). This is consistent with our finding of greater poverty reduction.

Second, in simulating the impact of policies we must make some assumption about the take-up of means-tested benefits and credits. The modelling takes account of non-take-up using estimates calculated by the Department for Work and Pensions.[10] As explained in more detail in Appendix III, this is necessarily done in an approximate way and may not reproduce the exact pattern of benefit (or tax credit) receipt that would be recorded in the survey data. However, the modelling does assume no change in take-up behaviour following a policy change. Thus any improvement in the take-up rate (or indeed any deterioration) that has been achieved over the period is not captured. We return to this issue in Chapter 4.

Other explanations relate to the use of the headcount poverty rate as the target measure. Increases in income only appear to be effective if they cause a child to cross from below the poverty line to above it. It may be combinations of factors that succeed in doing this even though each one of them contributes by increasing income to some extent. One cannot necessarily attribute poverty reduction (crossing the line) to any single factor. Taking different combinations of factors may result in different degrees of poverty reduction that are not necessarily proportional to their contribution. More generally, because of interactions between the various components we cannot say what share of poverty reduction is due to each factor. Indeed, the outcomes (crossing the line or not) may be quite different using BHC and AHC incomes.

Main findings

To summarise, we have found that:

- The direct effect of policy changes introduced between 1997 and 2003/4 is to reduce child poverty by about 1.3 million children, other things being equal. This is a proportional reduction of 30 per cent on an AHC basis.[11]

- On a BHC basis, the number of children removed from poverty is the same – 1.3 million – but because the 1997 rate of BHC poverty is lower than AHC poverty this represents a larger proportional reduction: 41 per cent.

- Other things did change, however. Allowing for real income growth over the period results in a smaller reduction – 1 million children using either the BHC or the AHC definition. On a BHC basis this represents a 33 per cent proportional reduction and on an AHC basis it is a 24 per cent reduction. These estimates assume no change in the composition of the population. Changes in employment, household composition and so on could have effects that either diminished the reduction or improved it.

- The room for uncertainty about the effects of such unmeasured changes can be reduced by taking estimates of actual child poverty reduction between 1996/7 and 2000/1 from Chapter 2 and adding the further reduction estimated for 2000/1 to 2003/4 using policy simulation, including the effects of real income growth. This results in an AHC estimate of 1.1 million (450,000 from Chapter 2 and 620,000 from Table 13) or almost exactly the target proportion of 25 per cent.[12] The BHC estimate is 0.9 million (540,000 from Chapter 2 and 330,000 from Table 13).

- Pensioner poverty on an AHC basis is significantly reduced by the policy changes introduced between 1997 and 2003/4, with most of the effect impacting after 2000/1. Allowing for income growth the poverty rate falls by 12 percentage points or a 45 per cent proportional reduction. Considering the policy changes alone, the proportional reduction is 60 per cent. Demographic changes (including population ageing), or other changes in household composition or labour market participation would affect these estimates.

- On a BHC basis there is a substantial fall in pensioner poverty due to policy changes using constant 2000/1 incomes – a 40 per cent proportional reduction or nearly 1 million taken out of poverty, other things being equal. The fall in pensioner poverty is much less using current incomes – a 13 per cent proportional reduction. This sensitivity to the poverty line and income measure is at least partly a result of the concentration of low income pensioners around particular levels of income corresponding to rates of benefit.

4 The sensitivity of ■ poverty estimates

The POLIMOD analysis has suggested a number of respects in which poverty estimates in general and those based on simulated incomes in particular may be very sensitive to certain assumptions. The underlying assumptions that underpin this sort of analysis deserve scrutiny if the estimates that have been presented are to be interpreted and made use of correctly.

First, there are some standard assumptions that are common to the kinds of calculations presented here, whether actual or simulated data are used. These are discussed below. We then discuss issues raised by the simulation process itself (page 42) and focus particularly on the statistical reliability of simulated estimates (page 44). Finally, we explore the robustness of results to the use of an alternative source of data: the Family Expenditure Survey, and draw conclusions.

The HBAI methodology

Equivalence scale

We have adopted the equivalence scale and the two income concepts (BHC and AHC) that are used in the official analysis of low income (see Appendix I). We are aware that different results would be obtained with a different choice of equivalence scale. For example, a scale which replicated the effective equivalence ratios in IS/MIG benefit rates would further concentrate people on benefit at the same point in the income distribution, particularly for AHC incomes. The position of the poverty line in relation to this income level would be even more crucial for the outcome.

The equivalence scale used here differs most notably from the commonly used OECD scale for very young children. This points to less poverty in families with very young children than would otherwise be recorded. It is not the purpose here to discuss the relative merits of different equivalence scales or to show the effects of using different scales. But the possible sensitivity of the results to the scale used should be borne in mind.

Choice of income concept

The use of two income concepts is itself inherently problematic. If we must use one – as is often the case with a specific target – which is better? What if they tell a different story? It is not even necessarily the case that the people in poverty or the people brought out of poverty are largely the same people under both definitions. Table 14 shows the children in and out of poverty in 2003/4 compared with 1997 using both definitions, based on the material shown in Table 13 (current incomes). This classifies children by their poverty status under the 1997 regime and shows what happens to that group under the 2003/4 regime. For example, 24 per cent of all children are classified as both BHC and AHC poor under the 1997 regime. Of these,

Table 14 Children classified as poor using BHC and AHC incomes under the policies and incomes in 1997 and 2003/4

Poverty classification under 1997 regime	Poverty classification under 2003/4 regime					% of all children under 1997 regime
	BHC and AHC	BHC only	AHC only	Neither	All cases	
BHC and AHC	64	3	18	15	100	23.8
BHC only	2	29	0	69	100	0.5
AHC only	2	0	55	43	100	9.6
Neither	~	~	~	99	100	66.1
All cases	15	1	10	74	100	100.0

Source: POLIMOD based on 1999/2000 Family Resources Survey data.

Note: Poverty is measured as the numbers of people living in households with equivalised income below 60 per cent of the within-scenario median. Figures are rounded to the nearest percentage point. This does not necessarily mean that estimates are statistically significant to the level shown. Columns may not add due to rounding.
~ indicates less than 0.5 per cent.

64 per cent remain both BHC and AHC poor under the 2003/4 regime. Fifteen per cent are brought out of both definitions of poverty, 18 per cent are no longer BHC poor but remain AHC poor and 3 per cent are BHC poor but no longer AHC poor. Thus, while the numbers of AHC poor are greater under both regimes it is not the case that all those BHC poor are also AHC poor.

About 10 per cent of all children were AHC poor but not BHC poor in the 1997 regime. Of these, 55 per cent remain in that state under 2003/4 policies, 43 per cent are no longer counted as poor at all and 2 per cent remain AHC poor and also move into being classified as BHC poor. We can summarise these figures as follows:

- The percentage reduction in child poverty defined on the basis of *both* BHC *and* AHC incomes is 38 per cent (from 24 per cent to 15 per cent).
- The percentage reduction in child poverty defined on the basis of *either* BHC *or* AHC incomes is 21 per cent (from 34 per cent to 27 per cent).

Simulation assumptions

The process of policy simulation involves making assumptions about how the rules governing benefit entitlement and tax liability actually work in practice and what assumptions to make about the 'counter-factual'. Here, we consider two important issues: non-take-up of benefits and the assumptions made in backdating and projecting mortgage interest payments.

Non-take-up

As explained in Appendix III, the simulations presented here are based on an assumption that non-take-up is random within broad groups who are each assumed to face the same probability of taking up their entitlement to each relevant benefit (or means-tested tax credit). This probability is independent of other personal or household characteristics or the size of the entitlement. Evidence suggests that take-up does in fact depend to some extent on the size of the entitlement (DSS 2000a). This would mean that although benefit receipt is modelled correctly on average the estimates presented here: (i) underestimate benefit amounts to some extent and (ii) may mis-allocate benefits to some people who do not take-up and fail to allocate benefits to people who would in fact successfully claim them. The impact of this on the poverty rates that we estimate is not possible to determine. By allocating too many small entitlements and too few large ones we may be pushing *either* too few *or* too many across the poverty line.

Since the main purpose is to simulate *changes* in policy we cannot simply tie take-up to evidence of benefit receipt recorded in the data. In the absence of a method to predict take-up behaviour of *each* of the UK means-tested benefits and credits we have preferred to rely on a simple method that is reasonably transparent in its effects.[13]

Updating assumptions: Mortgage interest

We have found that updating and backdating incomes to 2003/4 and 1997 has a significant effect on poverty rates and changes in them. The method used will therefore have an effect on results. There are two related difficulties. First, projections to 2003/4 are based on data from late 2002 or earlier plus projections based on growth in the latest period for which information is available. One exception is interest rates, which are assumed to stay at their latest rate (these are relevant to investment incomes and housing costs). Second, even where we have data for the relevant period (for example, 2000/1 back to 1997) it is not always clear how much of actual changes should be captured, given that compositional changes are not included in the analysis at all.

One example is how to account for changes in housing costs, particularly mortgage interest. Interest rates have been falling over the period. Thus someone with a certain mortgage debt in 2000/1 would have been paying more in 1997 for the same debt. But, on average, the real level of mortgage debt is growing. Our results depend on movements in both mortgage interest and total mortgage debt (see Appendix V). Using the interest rate alone would mean that our estimates of housing costs, particularly in 2003/4, would be much lower than 2003/4 data are likely to show. This would result in much larger growth in AHC incomes, an AHC poverty line that shifts up considerably and a fall in poverty rates that is less than our present estimates show. We can draw two conclusions from this. First, AHC poverty estimates based on simulations are particularly sensitive to assumptions about the housing market, which may not be very robust. BHC estimates are less sensitive and may therefore be preferable. Secondly, AHC estimates taken directly from data may be volatile due to fluctuations in the housing market and interest rates. This may be seen as an advantage –

they pick up short-term fluctuations in disposable income that are important to the people who experience them. But in that case it should be recognised that AHC measures have their ups and downs and that BHC measures have particular advantages in defining short-term targets and monitoring short-term developments.

Statistical reliability

Estimates based on survey data are always subject to sampling error. Published HBAI statistics are accompanied by confidence intervals and these are discussed in Chapter 2 in relation to estimates of changes in poverty using two separate samples. The estimates from POLIMOD use one sample but this does not mean that they are necessarily subject to less error. The reliability of policy simulation estimates of poverty (using 50 per cent mean income) following policy changes has been examined by Pudney and Sutherland (1994). They concluded: 'Poverty and inequality measures and aggregate benefit payments can have a wide margin of sampling error. This is particularly true for the effects of policy changes…' (pp. 345–6). While the sample they used was a quarter the size of the FRS, the poverty measure was based on the mean rather than the median and the policy changes with which they experimented were relatively small in impact, the general conclusion must still hold.

Choice of underlying data

Our analysis is based on Family Resources Survey (FRS), the same survey data that is used by HBAI. In the next chapter, where the additional effect of changes in indirect tax policies is examined, we make use of Family Expenditure Survey (FES) data. This data source contains information on household spending as well as income. Prior to 1994/5 it was this data source that was used as the basis for HBAI statistics. Since then FRS has been preferred because of its much larger sample size and more detailed questions on income. It remains of interest to establish what sort of poverty estimates are obtained using FES data. This enables us to link the findings on indirect tax in the next chapter to our earlier results for income poverty. It also provides us with an independent check on the robustness of the FRS-based results.

At the time of the change in data source for the official statistics some detailed comparisons of the sample characteristics and income variables in the two surveys were carried out. Frosztega et al. (2000) compared the HBAI datasets based on FES 1995/6 and FRS 1995/6 and found that BHC income was on average £6 a week lower in FRS than FES (Appendix Table 3). However, for some household types FES incomes were on average lower than FRS incomes. Using the same surveys Dayal et al. (2000) found that the income distributions of the two samples are statistically significantly different. These differences may result from a number of factors. First, there may be different patterns of non-response in the surveys due to different demands on respondents. The FRS is thought to better represent households in receipt of benefits (DSS 1997; Appendix 9), which is consistent with the lower average incomes in that survey. Studies of non-respondents in the two surveys reported in Frosztega et al. (2000) suggest that FRS over-represents some types of low-income household and under-represents some types of high-income household. In contrast, FES appears to under-represent people living in council flats and over-represent those with mortgages and those living in rural areas.

Table 15 Policy simulation estimates of poverty under policy regimes of 1997, 2000/1 and 2003/4, using current incomes in 2000/1 prices and Family Expenditure Survey data

	All		Children		Children in 2 parent families		Children in 1 parent families		People over pension age	
	Number (000)	Rate (%)	Number (000)	Rate (%)	Number (000)	Rate (%)	Number (000)	Rate (%)	Number (000)	Rate (%)
(1) BHC 1997 regime	11,160	19	3,500	26	2,180	21	1,320	41	1,980	20
(2) BHC 2000/1 regime	9,980	17	2,810	21	1,830	18	980	30	1,860	18
(3) BHC 2003/4 regime	9,430	16	2,510	18	1,620	16	890	27	1,770	17
Reduction (1)–(2)	1,190	2	690	5	350	3	340	11	120	1
Reduction (2)–(3)	550	1	300	2	210	2	100	3	100	1
Reduction (1)–(3)	1,730	3	990	7	560	5	440	13	220	2
(1) AHC 1997 regime	14,680	25	4,630	34	2,620	25	2,010	62	2,600	26
(2) AHC 2000/1 regime	13,400	23	4,080	30	2,330	23	1,750	54	2,320	23
(3) AHC 2003/4 regime	11,940	20	3,680	27	1,990	19	1,690	52	1,660	16
Reduction (1)–(2)	1,280	2	550	4	290	3	260	8	290	3
Reduction (2)–(3)	1,460	2	400	3	340	3	60	2	650	6
Reduction (1)–(3)	2,740	5	940	7	630	6	320	10	940	9

Source: POLIMOD based on 2000/1 Family Expenditure Survey data.

Note: The GB data is reweighted to match the same control totals (family composition, Council Tax band, housing tenure, London/not London) as used in FRS 2000/1 for HBAI. N. Ireland households retain their FES weights which are based on age and sex categories only.

Note : Poverty is measured as the numbers of people living in households with equivalised income below 60 per cent of the within-scenario median. Figures are rounded to the nearest 10,000 persons or

Second, the criteria for inclusion in the sample as a responding household are more stringent in the FES than the FRS and the methods of imputation of missing values in the two surveys are different. Third, the FES household was in fact a 'spending unit' but has been treated as though it were the same as the FRS 'household'. In fact the former is a narrower unit, conditional on there being some common housekeeping including meal preparation. Some FRS households would thus be treated as separate units in the FES. Since these tend to be young adults sharing accommodation (usually private rented), this is likely to increase the proportion of multi-adult 'households' and decrease the proportion of single adult 'households' in the FRS compared to the FES.

It is difficult to say – without carrying out another in-depth study – whether these differences apply in the same way to more recent surveys. However, there are other differences in the two sources (accounted for in the comparisons described above). The sample size is very different: FRS contains around 25,000 households and the FES around 6,500. FES covers Northern Ireland as well as Great Britain and FRS includes more detailed questions about income. Although it is not possible to reproduce the FRS income definition used in HBAI exactly, broadly comparable BHC and AHC income variables have been used to reproduce the analysis in Table 13 using FES for 2000/1, in Table 15. The basic methodology is the same and the methods of backdating to 1997 and projection to 2003/4 use the same principles as described in Appendix V.

In the calculations in Table 15 we make use of one device to align the results for FES to those from FRS. The original FES data use weights calculated on the basis of region, age and sex alone. They have been re-calculated for Great Britain using the population control totals that are used to construct weights for the FRS in 2000/1.[14] Weights for Northern Ireland take their original values.

The results are quite similar to those obtained from FRS for the previous year. In particular:

- Poverty rates under the 1997 regime for all groups and on both the BHC and AHC bases are the same or slightly higher (no more than 2 percentage points) using FES. The exception is pensioners, whose poverty rates are slightly lower (1 percentage point) using FES.
- The changes in poverty between the 1997 and 2003/4 regimes are also similar. With the exception of children in one-parent families and pensioners using the AHC definition there is no more than 1 percentage point difference in the estimates of the fall in poverty rate using the two data sources.
- On an AHC basis the fall in poverty for children in one-parent families is 10 percentage points using FES compared with 15 using FRS. For pensioners the reduction is 9 percentage points rather than 12 using FRS. As we have seen, the poverty rate is very sensitive to the precise position of the poverty line in relation to the mode of the income distribution for these groups. Lack of robustness across data sources in these measures is not therefore very surprising.

Concluding points

In drawing conclusions about changes in poverty rates using policy simulation methods it is important to remember:

- The AHC and BHC measures may tell a different story. Both sets of results are informative and one should not (generally) be preferred over the other.
- The AHC measure tends to result in higher poverty rates although this is not necessarily the case for pensioners. But not all the BHC poor are also AHC poor.
- Income distributions of certain groups – particularly those living on Income Support – may be highly concentrated, particularly when using AHC measures of income. This means that poverty rates may be very sensitive to the precise position of the poverty line.
- AHC measures are particularly sensitive to movements in mortgage interest payments and to the assumptions that are made about them.
- Estimates based on different datasets may not be identical. The comparison between FRS and FES shown here suggests that the main sensitivities arise from differing levels of poverty line rather than any major difference in the composition of the poor or those removed from poverty.
- To some extent the necessarily crude assumptions that are made about take-up of means-tested benefits will have a bearing on the results. We cannot make a judgement about the direction of any bias in the estimated poverty rates, or changes to them.

5 Distributional effects of changes in indirect tax policy, 1997–2002/3

Introduction

As part of understanding the distributional impact of this government's policies, it is important to consider changes in indirect taxes, as well as direct tax and benefit policies. Indirect taxes make up a substantial proportion of the total tax base and are more regressive than direct taxes. Hence, changes in indirect taxes (and the balance between direct and indirect taxation) could potentially alter our conclusions about the distributional impact of recent fiscal policies.

In estimating the effect of recent changes in indirect tax policies, based on the Family Expenditure Survey,[15] expenditure patterns are held constant at 2000/1 levels. More specifically, we estimate how much less or more each household would pay in indirect taxes if they bought the same package of goods as in 2000/1, but at the rates of duty/tax that prevailed in May 1997 or 2002/3, adjusted for inflation. By holding expenditure patterns constant, our estimates are designed to capture the 'pure' effect of policy changes. As with direct taxes and benefits, there will have been other changes which affect the actual amount of indirect taxes paid by households beyond these 'pure policy' effects. More specifically, our estimates do not capture the effects of changes in patterns of consumer spending over this period due to rising incomes, changing tastes, or changes in indirect tax rates themselves (for example, people smoking less because of increases in tobacco duties). This is consistent with the first approach used to simulate the effect of direct tax and benefit changes in Chapter 3 (see page 25).

In 2000/1, net revenue from indirect taxes in the UK was around £120 billion, of which around £80 billion was borne directly by UK households (see Table 16). This £80bn figure, which is the focus of this chapter, excludes indirect taxes paid by producers on the inputs used in the production of final goods and passed on to consumers. It also excludes an estimate of payments by households not resident in the UK. The largest single item was Value Added Tax (VAT), which accounted for just under 60 per cent of the total. Other major items were duties on petrol, alcohol and tobacco, which together accounted for around 30 per cent of net receipts. The remainder was made up of a number of special taxes on specific products, such as betting taxes and stamp duty.

The rest of this section provides a brief description of each these taxes and how they have changed since 1997. Rates of tax/duty are summarised in Table 17.

Table 16 Total payment of indirect taxes by UK households in 2000/1

Duty/tax	Total net revenue[1] (£ million)	Amount borne directly by UK households[2] (£ million)	% of total
Value Added Tax	58,621	47,812	58
Duty on hydrocarbon oils[3]	22,623	10,481	13
Duty on tobacco	7,648	7,055	9
Duty on alcoholic drinks	6,663	5,829	7
Vehicle excise duty	4,300	3,222	4
Betting duties	3,006	2,929	4
TV licence fee	2,555	2,555	3
Stamp duty on house purchase	8,165	1,620	2
Insurance premium tax	1,707	849	1
Air passenger duty	949	492	0.6
Total	**116,237**	**82,844**	**100**

Notes: 1 Revenue totals for most taxes are from Table A1 of HM Customs and Excise's Annual Report, which is available online (HM Customs and Excise 2003). Revenue from Vehicle Excise Duty is from the Budget Report 2002. Revenue from stamp duties is from Table T1.2 ('Annual Receipts of Inland Revenue Taxes') available on the Inland Revenue's website (www.inlandrevenue.gov.uk/stats/ tax_receipts/g_t02_1.htm).
2 Estimates for most taxes were provided by the Office for National Statistics, except for VAT, Vehicle Excise Duty and TV licence fees, which were imputed using information on expenditure and car/TV ownership from the 2000/01 Family Expenditure Survey.
3 Excluding duty on oil for central heating or lubricating oil (£8m), and hydrocarbons used in public transport (£534m).

Value Added Tax

The standard rate of VAT is 17.5 per cent, although certain goods, such as children's clothes, are zero-rated or exempt, and some items, notably domestic fuel, are subject to a reduced rate – currently set at 5 per cent. It is estimated that just over half of all consumers' expenditure is taxable at the standard rate and 3 per cent is taxed at the reduced rate (Adam and Kaplan 2002). For the purposes of this analysis, we only count the tax paid on the price of final goods sold to consumers, although VAT is also paid on the inputs used to produce these goods – part of which will in practice be passed on to consumers in higher prices.

The standard rate has remained at 17.5 per cent since 1997. The reduced rate on domestic fuel, which was introduced in 1994–5, was reduced from 8 per cent to 5 per cent in 1997, shortly after Labour came into power. More recently, a number of smaller items have also been added to the list of reduced-rated items, including children's car seats and women's sanitary products.

Table 17 Rates of tax/duty

Tax/duty	Prevailing rate in current prices:			% change (in real terms)[1]	
	May 1997	April 2000	April 2002	1997– 2000/1	1997– 2002/3
VAT					
standard rate	17.5%	17.5%	17.5%	+1%[2]	+1%[2]
reduced rate	8%	5%	5%	−38%	−38%
Hydrocarbon oils					
petrol (pence per litre)[3]	38.43	48.99	45.95	+17%	+6%
diesel (pence per litre)[4]	36.86	48.83	45.84	+21%	+10%
Vehicle excise duty	145	155	160	−2%	−3%
Cigarettes					
ad valorem	21%	22%	22%		
specific (£ per 1,000)	65.97	90.43	94.24		
total duty (per 20)[5]	213.72	267.81	269.11	+25%	+26%
Alcohol					
beer (per 1% ABV)	10.82	11.89	11.89	+1%	−3%
still wine (£ per hectolitre)	140.44	154.37	154.37	+1%	−3%
spirits (£ per litre)	18.99	19.56	19.56	−6%	−9%
General betting duty	6.75% (of stakes)	6.75% (of stakes)	15% (of profits)	0%	–
Stamp duty					
60–250,000	1%	1%	1%	0%	0%
250–500,000	1%	3%	3%	+200%	+200%
500,000+	1%	4%	4%	+300%	+300%
Insurance premium tax	4%	5%	5%	+25%	+25%
Air passenger duty					
rates	£5–£10	£10–£20	£5–£40		
average[6]	6.40	12.80	10.15	+83%	+40%
TV licence fee					
full fee	91.50	104.00	112.00[7]	+4%	+8%

Notes: 1 Adjusted to 2000/1 prices using the all items Retail Price Index. Rates in May 1997 are inflated by 9.2 per cent and rates in April 2002 are deflated by 3.5 per cent.

2 Although the standard rate of VAT has remained constant, VAT charges on standard rated items have effectively increased because additional VAT is being paid on the increase in duties on alcohol, tobacco and petrol.

3 Weighted average of duties for leaded, unleaded, super unleaded and ultra-low sulphur petrol, using volumes purchased in each year as weights.

4 As above, but based on duties for DERV and ultra-low sulphur diesel.

5 Based on original price (net of tax) of 69 pence per pack of 20.

6 Weighted average based on volumes of air traffic by destination and class of travel (in 2001/2).

7 Those aged 75 and over are now exempt– just under 10% of households with TVs.

Excise duties

Petrol, diesel, alcohol and tobacco products are subject to specific duties, as well as VAT. In all but one case, these duties are fixed in nominal terms (i.e. so many pence per litre or kilogram). Rates are typically up-rated each year to allow for inflation, although some rates may be frozen (in nominal terms) or raised by more than the rate of inflation, in some cases as part of stated government policy (e.g. the fuel duty escalator, which operated for much of the 1990s). Differential rates are often set, for example to reflect the alcohol content of the product or, in the case of low-sulphur petrol and vehicle excise duty, to create incentives for consumers to switch to more environmentally friendly fuel or cars. Cigarettes are subject both to a specific (or fixed) duty and an *ad valorem* duty – currently at 22 per cent – as well as VAT.

Since 1997, the rates on alcoholic drinks have fallen slightly in real terms, more so on spirits. The effective duties on most tobacco products have risen significantly in real terms – by over 25 per cent on cigarettes. The story for petrol and diesel is more complex, because of changes in the composition of sales. Up to 2000/1, the duty on petrol and diesel rose significantly in real terms – by 17 per cent and 21 per cent respectively. In April 2002, the rates on ultra-low sulphur petrol and diesel were cut (by around 10 per cent in real terms) and these now account for most sales, offsetting some of the increases in previous years.

Other indirect taxes

In addition to VAT and excise duties, there are a number of other indirect taxes on specific products. In order of importance (in terms of net receipts), these are:

- *Betting and gaming duties* These used to be levied as a fixed percentage of gross stakes, but from January 2002 are in most cases levied as a (higher) fixed percentage of estimated profits.
- *TV licence* There is a fixed fee per household – currently £112. Since November 2001, those aged 75 or over are exempt.
- *Stamp duty* Payable by house buyers on the purchase price of their home. This used to be a fixed percentage (1 per cent) of the purchase price, but now higher rates (up to 4 per cent) are charged on more expensive properties.
- *Insurance premium tax* Levied at a standard rate of 5 per cent of gross premiums on most general insurance products (e.g. motor, travel and medical insurance), excluding life insurance and other long-term insurance products.
- *Air passenger duty* A fixed charge on passengers travelling from UK airports. Rates are higher for travel outside the European Economic Area (EEA) and/or for those travelling first or club class.

Many of these taxes have been increased in recent years, albeit from a fairly low tax base. Higher rates of stamp duty were introduced for more expensive properties (see above), the insurance premium tax was increased from 4 per cent to 5 per cent and air passenger duties were doubled in November 1997 (although the latter increase was partly reversed in the restructuring that took place in April 2001).

Estimating the distributional effects of indirect taxation

The base year for our analysis is 2000/1, the latest year for which we have expenditure data from the Family Expenditure Survey (FES). For most taxes, total revenue for each tax is allocated between households in proportion to their reported expenditure on relevant items. For example, a household that spends £20 per week on cigarettes is assumed to pay twice as much in cigarette duties as one that spends £10 per week. By allocating total tax revenue in this way, we automatically allow for the fact that, on average, people under-report their expenditure on items like tobacco and alcohol. (The implicit assumption is that the degree of under-reporting is the same for all types of household.)

Value Added Tax and stamp duty are treated differently. For VAT, we identify those items that are subject to VAT, adjust certain items to allow for under-reporting of expenditure,[16] and work out how much of that spending comprises VAT.[17] Certain items that are now subject to the reduced-rate of VAT, such as children's car seats and women's sanitary products, cannot be identified separately in the FES data set, so they are treated no differently from other standard-rated items. However, the amounts involved are likely to be very small relative to total VAT payments.

Stamp duty is paid by house-buyers on the purchase price of the property. This is a relatively small proportion of households in any given year and the FES sample of recent homebuyers is correspondingly small. Rather than allocating stamp duty payments to these households, payments are spread across all mortgagors, based on the probability of them moving home in any given year, which in turn is a function of their age and family type.[18] The amount they would pay if they moved home is equal to the rate of stamp duty multiplied by the imputed value of their current property.[19]

Having estimated indirect tax payments in 2000/1, we simulate the effect of recent changes in indirect tax policies, holding expenditure patterns constant (i.e. as they were in 2000/1). In other words, how much less or more would each household be paying in indirect taxes if they bought the same package of goods but at the same rates of duty/tax that prevailed in May 1997 and, projecting forwards, if they faced the rates of duty/tax prevailing in 2002/3. Rates of tax/duty are adjusted for inflation over this period so, for example, it is possible for a specific duty to have risen in nominal terms, but to have fallen in real terms. By holding expenditure patterns constant, our estimates are designed to capture the 'pure' effect of policy changes. If, instead, we estimated actual indirect tax payments in 1997, 2000/1, and 2002/3, then we would be picking up the effect of changes in patterns of consumer spending over the period, as well as policy changes. Rising incomes over time are not taken into account either. Spending rises with incomes, so we would expect households to pay more in indirect taxes as they become better off, but less as a proportion of their incomes (because most indirect taxes are regressive). Thus, allowing for income growth would be expected to reduce the burden of indirect taxation in later years relative to earlier years.

Information on rates of duty/tax on most products are taken from HM Customs and Excise's Annual Report and adjusted to 2000/1 prices using the all items retail price index (HM Customs and Excise 2003). We have not attempted to estimate the distributional impact of changes in betting duties, because of reforms to the tax system, which make it very difficult to make comparisons between the beginning and end of the period.

Incidence of indirect taxes

This section examines the incidence of indirect taxes in 2000/1 – the base year for our analysis. It provides a breakdown of tax payments by income group and family type and looks at how regressive different types of indirect tax are. The next section considers the overall distributional impact of recent changes in indirect tax rates and provides a more detailed analysis of gainers and losers. The final section examines the impact of these changes on rates of poverty.

Figure 11 shows total indirect tax payments by decile group (based on households' disposable income before housing costs, adjusted for household size). Households in lower income groups pay less than half the amount of indirect taxes paid by higher income groups, because spending on most taxable items increases with households' incomes. But indirect tax payments are regressive: they represent a much higher proportion of poorer households' incomes, especially for those in the bottom decile group. This is because they report spending more in relation to their incomes and because, on average, a higher share of their expenditure is on more heavily taxed goods, such as tobacco.

Some indirect taxes are more regressive than others. Table 18 compares the amount paid in tax by the bottom and top quintile groups for different types of tax/duty. The most regressive

Figure 11 **Total indirect tax payments by income group**

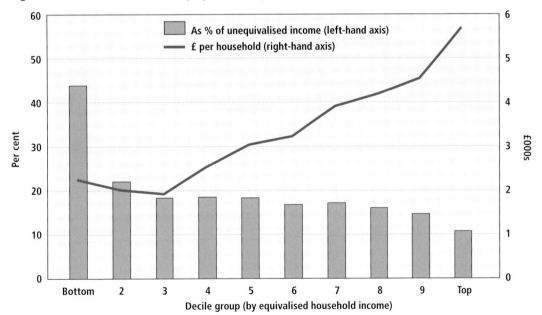

Table 18 Distributional impact of different indirect taxes

Tax/duty	Average tax paid (£/year)		Ratio of tax paid by bottom and top quintiles	
	Bottom quintile	Top quintile		
Tobacco duty	298	243	1.2	
TV licence fee	104	105	1.0	
Betting tax	91	120	0.8	
Alcohol duty	138	363	0.4	Regressive
VAT	1,136	3,158	0.4	
Motoring taxes (inc. VED)	298	847	0.4	
Insurance premium tax	18	60	0.3	
Stamp duty	30	167	0.2	Neutral
Air passenger duty	8	44	0.2	
Average	**2,119**	**5,104**	**0.4**	

Figure 12 **Indirect tax payments by family type**

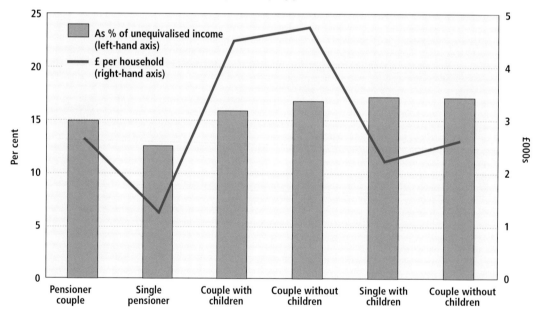

are tobacco duty, the TV licence fee and betting taxes. Alcohol duties, motoring taxes, VAT and the insurance premium tax are moderately regressive, while stamp duty and air passenger duty are broadly neutral, that is, tax payments are more or less proportional to household income (net household incomes for those in the bottom income group are, on average, a fifth of those in the top income group).

Figure 12 shows indirect tax payments by family type. The most notable difference is between pensioner households, especially single pensioners, and other family types. Single pensioners spend less of their income and more of what they spend is on tax-exempt items, so they pay

Family type	£ per year	% of income
Pensioner couple	1,681	20.2
Single pensioner	839	17.0
Couple with children	3,187	30.2
Couple without children	3,746	50.7
Single with children	1,825	21.9
Single without children	1,855	40.5
All households	**2,118**	**29.7**

Table 19 **Indirect tax payments by family type, bottom quintile group**[1]

Note: 1 Poorest fifth of all households, based on net equivalised household incomes before housing costs.

less in VAT as a proportion of their income; they also travel less, drink less and move home less often than other households.

We might have expected lone parents, the majority of whom have relatively low incomes, to be paying a much higher proportion of their income in indirect taxes than other non-pensioner households, given that indirect taxes are regressive. On average, however, they pay around the same proportion of their income in indirect taxes as other non-pensioner households. And, compared with other households on low incomes, lone parents and pensioners pay a substantially smaller share of their incomes in indirect taxes (see Table 19). One reason is that, like pensioners, they tend to drink less, travel less and move house less frequently than other households on similar incomes. Lone parents and pensioners are also more likely to be in persistent poverty (Gardiner and Hills 1999), so they may be less able to maintain spending levels that are high relative to their incomes (unlike households that may only be experiencing a relatively short spell of low income).

As already noted, the amount households pay in tax depends on their spending patterns. The amounts given above show averages for different income groups or family types, but there will be a lot of variation within these groups, for example between households with smokers and those without. Table 20 shows that the proportion of income spent on indirect taxes varies hugely depending on people's drinking, smoking and driving habits, especially among poorer households – by a factor of up to three among low income single pensioners and lone parents. So, although indirect taxes are, on average, regressive (i.e. low income households pay a higher proportion of their income in taxes than higher income households), there are even greater differences between households who smoke, drink and own cars compared with those who do not. The third column shows the impact of changes in indirect tax rates, which are discussed in the following section.

Table 20 Variation in indirect tax payments

	Average paid in indirect taxes (£/year)	Tax as % of h/hold income	Impact of tax changes as % of income: 1997–2002/3
Low income single pensioner	**867**	**15**	**−0.3**
Car-owners	1,518	26	+0.2
Non-car-owners	679	11	−0.4
Smokers	1,830	26	+1.8
Non-smokers	669	12	−0.8
Drinkers	1,241	20	0.0
Non-drinkers	702	12	−0.4
At least two of the above	1,952	29	+1.1
None of the above	436	8	−1.0
Low income lone parent	**1,872**	**20**	**+0.9**
Car-owners	2,691	27	+1.0
Non-car-owners	1,349	15	+0.9
Smokers	2,316	24	+1.8
Non-smokers	1,502	16	+0.1
Drinkers	2,143	22	+0.9
Non-drinkers	1,619	17	+1.0
At least two of the above	2,640	26	+1.3
One or none of the above	1,229	13	+0.6
Low income couple with children	**3,321**	**25**	**+1.0**
Car-owners	3,657	27	+1.0
Non-car-owners	2,146	17	+1.0
Smokers	3,614	26	+1.5
Non-smokers	2,978	23	+0.4
Drinkers	3,742	27	+1.0
Non-drinkers	2,559	21	+1.0
At least two of the above	3,772	27	+1.2
One or none of the above	2,117	18	+0.5
Mid income couple with children	**4,174**	**17**	**+0.4**
Car-owners	4,223	17	+0.4
Non-car-owners	*	*	*
Smokers	4,866	20	+0.9
Non-smokers	3,772	15	+0.1
Drinkers	4,297	18	+0.4
Non-drinkers	3,669	15	+0.6
All the above	5,117	21	+0.9
One or none of the above	3,405	14	+0.3
High income couple, no children	**5,464**	**14**	**+0.4**
Car-owners	5,529	14	+0.4
Non-car-owners	*	*	*
Smokers	6,325	17	+0.7
Non-smokers	5,052	13	+0.2
Drinkers	5,706	15	+0.3
Non-drinkers	3,810	11	+0.4
All the above	6,590	17	+0.7
One or none of the above	3,654	9	+0.2

Notes: * Results not reported because of sample is too small (cell size of less than 100).
Low income, mid income and high income means households with net equivalised household incomes (BHC) in the bottom, middle or top third of the distribution for all households, respectively.

Distributional effects of recent changes in indirect tax rates

Recent changes in indirect taxes are summarised in Table 21. There have been substantial rises (in real terms) in tobacco duties and a number of the smaller taxes – stamp duty, insurance premium tax and air passenger duty. Motoring taxes rose during Labour's first term in office, but much of this has been reversed in the last two years. Other indirect taxes have also been cut in real terms since 2000/1, including alcohol duties and TV licence fees for people over 75 years of age. The incidence of VAT has remained broadly constant as the reduced rate for domestic fuel and power has been more or less cancelled out by the knock-on effect of higher excise duties on VAT, which is charged on the price of goods inclusive of duties.

The distributional impact of these changes is shown in Figure 13. Holding spending patterns constant, all income groups are paying more in indirect taxes as a result of the policies implemented since 1997, but this increase is greatest (as a proportion of their income) for poorer households. This is not surprising, given that most indirect taxes are regressive. Taken as a whole, the indirect tax system has become neither more nor less regressive over the period 1997–2002/3. Other things being equal, substantial rises in tobacco duties – the most regressive tax – would have made the system more regressive, but this has been offset by above-average increases in the least regressive taxes (namely stamp duty, insurance tax and air passenger duty).

Recent changes have affected family types differently (see Figure 14). Pensioners have been relatively unaffected by changes in indirect tax policies, largely because increases in excise duties have been offset by exempting people over 75 from the TV licence fee, which is worth over £100 per year. Lone parents have been hit hardest, because they spend a relatively high

---

Table 21 **The impact of changes in indirect tax rates, 1997–2002/3**

| | Net change in burden of indirect taxes[1] (£ per household/year) | | | |
	1997–2000/1	2000/1–2002/3	Total	As % of each tax in 1997[2]
VAT	3	−8	−5	−0.3
Tobacco duty	56	1	58	25.6
Alcohol duty	−3	−8	−12	−4.9
Motoring taxes	60	−41	19	3.9
Stamp duty	19	0	19	40.1
Insurance tax	7	0	7	25.5
Air passenger duty	9	−5	4	40.7
TV licence	4	−5	−1	−0.5
Total	**155**	**−66**	**89**	**2.8**

Notes: 1 Holding spending constant at 2000/1 levels.
　　　2 Imputed on basis of 1997 rates and 2000/1 expenditure patterns.

Figure 13 **Impact of changes in indirect tax rates by income group, 1997–2002/3**

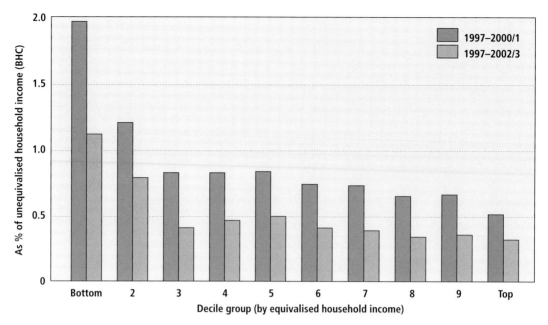

Figure 14 **Impact of changes in indirect tax rates by family type, 1997-2002/3**

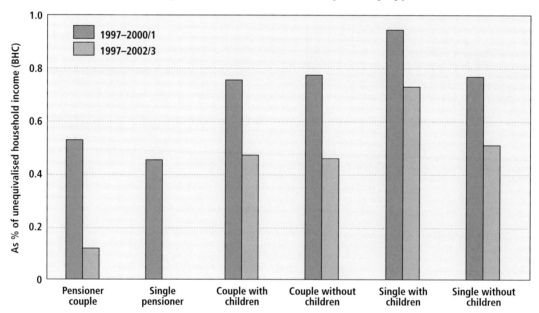

share of their budget on tobacco, which has seen the largest rise in excise duties. There is even greater variation between individual households, in particular between smokers and non-smokers (see final column of Table 20). For low income lone parents who smoke, the impact of changes in indirect tax rates between 1997–2002/3 is equivalent to a net loss in average household income of nearly 2 percentage points. At the other extreme, low income pensioners who do not smoke experience a net gain equivalent to around 1 percentage point of their income, on average.

Impact on poverty rates

The income definition on which the government's official measure of poverty is based does not take into account indirect taxation. (Households are ranked according to their net equivalised household income, after deducting direct taxes but before deducting indirect tax payments.) Changes in indirect tax rates will thus not show up in standard measures of poverty, including those reported in previous chapters. In order to be able to put into context the effect of recent changes in indirect tax rates, we worked out how much poverty rates would have changed if there had been an equivalent change in direct taxation (which would be captured in official poverty measures). The purpose of this exercise is to give an order of magnitude for the impact of indirect tax changes, which may be compared against the impact of direct tax and benefit changes. As in previous chapters, the effect of policies on the poverty line itself is taken into account in these estimates.

On this basis, Table 22 shows the equivalent impact on poverty rates of changes in indirect taxes announced since 1997. The final column suggests that, other things being equal, overall poverty rates would have been marginally higher on this basis – and hence poverty reductions smaller – by around 0.4 percentage points. This is because low income households pay a disproportionate share of their income in indirect taxes, so the equivalent of these changes if they had affected disposable incomes would have pushed more households below the poverty line (even though the poverty line itself falls). For lone-parent households, who are worst affected by these changes, the impact is equivalent to a rise of more than 1 percentage point in the poverty rate, although this is still relatively small compared to the 5 percentage point reduction in poverty that lone-parent households experienced between 1996/7–2000/1 (see Chapter 2). Poverty rates for pensioners and single person households are virtually unaffected by changes in indirect taxes over this period.

Table 22 Equivalent impact on poverty rates of changes in indirect tax rates[1]

	Net effect of policy change: 1997–2002/3 (Change in % of households below 60% of median incomes[2])
Pensioner couple	+0.2
Single pensioner	+0.2
Couple with children	+0.5
Couple without children	+0.5
Single with children	+1.2
Single without children	+0.1
All households with children	**+0.6**
All pensioner households	**+0.2**
All persons	**+0.4**

Notes: 1 If households' disposable incomes changed by an amount equivalent to the impact of changing tax rates on their indirect tax payments.
2 Allowing for the impact of the indirect tax adjustment on median incomes.

Summary

This chapter has examined the incidence of indirect taxes and the distributional impact of changes in the indirect tax system implemented since 1997, holding expenditure patterns constant. Indirect taxes as a whole are regressive – poorer households pay a higher proportion of their income in indirect taxes than richer households – but some are more regressive than others. The most regressive taxes are tobacco duty, the TV licence fee and betting taxes. Alcohol duties, motoring taxes, VAT and insurance premium tax are moderately regressive, while stamp duty and air passenger duty are broadly neutral. Although indirect taxes are, on average, regressive, there are even greater differences between households who smoke, drink and own cars compared with those who do not. Compared with other family types, single pensioners pay significantly less of their incomes in indirect taxes.

On balance, indirect taxes and duties have increased in real terms since 1997 (though they fell between 2000/1 and 2002/3). This will have affected poorer households disproportionately, because most indirect taxes are regressive. Lone-parent households are hardest hit by the above-average increase in tobacco duties, while pensioners are least affected, largely because over 75-year-olds have been exempted from TV licence fees.

If the distributional effects of changes in indirect taxes were reflected in the official poverty measure, overall poverty rates would have been marginally higher – and reported reduction in poverty less – as a result of changes in indirect taxation since 1997. For lone-parent households, who have been most adversely affected, the impact of higher indirect tax rates is equivalent to an increase in their poverty rate of around one percentage point.

All the estimates in this chapter are based on expenditure patterns in 2000/1. Further research would be needed to examine the possible impact of any changes in pattern consumer spending over the period 1997–2002/3, including the impact of tax changes on consumer behaviour.

6 Conclusions ■

Answers depend on questions

A major lesson learned from carrying out the sort of analysis described here is that it is very important to clearly state the question that the analysis is attempting to address. To illustrate this there follows a series of slightly different questions about movements in child and pensioner poverty over the period 1997 to 2003/4. In each case the answer is presented based on income before and after housing costs (BHC and AHC). For each question these answers differ because the extent of poverty is different on the two measures and policy changes have somewhat different effects. The questions (and the answers to them) use different: (i) choices of base year – this affects the initial poverty lines and poverty rates; and (ii) assumptions about whether pre-tax and benefit income changes are included in the calculations, as well as the effect of policy changes.

A *If there had been no changes to the direct tax and benefit system since 1997 (except indexation for inflation) how much higher would poverty rates be in 2003/4 than under the 2003/4 system?*

	Children		Pensioners	
	BHC	AHC	BHC	AHC
Proportional increase in 2003/4 poverty rate (%)	62	38	53	129
Increase in number in poverty (thousands)	1,300	1,200	1,000	1,900

Assuming 2003/4 incomes; 1999/2000 composition; no second order effects
Source: Additional calculations using POLIMOD

B *What effect has the government's tax and benefit policy changes (1997–2003/4) had on poverty?*

	Children		Pensioners	
	BHC	AHC	BHC	AHC
Proportional reduction in poverty (%)	41	30	39	60
Fall in number in poverty (thousands)	1,300	1,300	1,000	1,800

Assuming 2000/1 prices and incomes; 1999/2000 composition; no second order effects
Source: Table 12

The difference in the percentage changes in the answers to questions A and B is due to the different starting points (A considers percentage increases; B percentage reductions). The (small) differences in numbers brought into or out of poverty are due to the different base income levels (A uses 2003/4 incomes and B uses 2000/1 incomes).

The answer we have supplied to question B relates to direct tax and benefit changes (as in question A). If changes in indirect tax policy were included then the reduction in poverty rates would be lower by the following proportions:

| | Children | | Pensioners | |
	BHC	AHC	BHC	AHC
Proportional change in poverty (%)	+3	+3	+1	-1

Assuming 2000/1 expenditure patterns and applying the tax changes as though they were equivalent changes in direct taxes.
Source: Table 22

C How much will poverty fall between 1997–2003/4?

We cannot know for certain. Assuming no compositional changes and allowing for the direct effect of policy changes and expected real growth in incomes we can estimate:

| | Children | | Pensioners | |
	BHC	AHC	BHC	AHC
Proportional reduction in poverty (%)	33	24	13	45
Fall in number in poverty (thousands)	1,000	1,000	300	1,200

Assuming current incomes in 2000/1 prices; 1999/2000 composition; no second order effects
Source: Table 13

The answer to question C differs from that for question B because changes in real pre-tax and benefit incomes between 1997 and 2003/4 are taken into account in C.

D Will the government meet its target to reduce child poverty by 25 per cent by 2004?

We do not know. Assuming no adverse changes (such as lower employment) since 1999/2000, no direct policy changes that increase poverty (by reducing low incomes or inflating the poverty line) and allowing only for the direct effect of policy changes and real growth in incomes we can use the answer to question C to answer this question. This suggests the target could be met.

Our estimate is thus that child poverty will be about a quarter below its 1998/9 level by 2004, in line with the government's target, unless other factors change in an unfavourable direction in which case more redistributive measures will be needed. That would be a significant achievement.

What then are the prospects beyond 2003/4?

For poverty to remain at the same level, let alone fall, it is necessary both for employment to be maintained and for benefits and tax credits to keep up with median incomes. This necessarily requires more expenditure in real terms, although not more as a proportion of national income. In terms of overall poverty, it remains the case that Income Support levels are substantially below the government's own poverty level. The failure in recent years to increase these levels in line with median incomes has made this situation worse. The government's own goal of 'security for those who cannot work' is a long way from being achieved.

The findings of this study show the challenge that tackling poverty represents. Between 1996/7 and 2000/1 relative poverty fell, largely as a result of improvements in employment rates and in the level of some benefits. But the overall impact was modest when compared to a poverty line that rose with median incomes. The tax and benefit changes analysed in the study do have a major effect – but once again much of this is needed simply to keep up with a moving target.

What the study shows is that greater employment, or 'work for those who can', has made a real contribution to reducing poverty. But there is a limit to the amount of employment increases that are possible. The study also shows that without the improvements which have been made to the tax and benefit system for those with low incomes, poverty would be much worse. Changes in indirect taxation have had only a small effect on poverty but it is important for the future that their regressive effects are taken into account. Whatever its form, more redistribution will be needed each year simply to maintain the progress which has been made.

In 1999 a goal was set of halving child poverty by 2010 and a relative definition of poverty was clearly adopted. Even if this goal is achieved, relative poverty will still be higher than in 1979. It will be possible to stay on track to achieve this goal but to do so will require substantially more redistribution to the poorest and continuing priority to be given to the goal of ending child poverty. Further reductions in child poverty are likely to be increasingly hard to achieve. Beyond child poverty, the task of ending poverty more generally remains to be tackled. Britain at the beginning of the twenty-first century remains a nation scarred by poverty.

Appendix I ∎
Methods, data and assumptions

Households Below Average Income statistics

Household Below Average Income (HBAI) statistics are published annually, based on data from the Family Resources Survey. The main income measures are 'Before Housing Costs (BHC)' and 'After Housing Costs (AHC)'. The BHC income definition includes, for all members of the household:

- usual earnings
- self-employment income
- social security benefits, pensions and credits (but not social fund loans)
- income from occupational and personal pensions
- investment income
- maintenance payments, educational grants and scholarships (including student loans) and transfers from family members outside the household
- imputed cash value of free school meals, free welfare and school milk
- less: income tax, National Insurance contributions, council tax, contributions to private pensions, maintenance and child support payments and payments to students living outside the household.

The AHC income definition deducts gross rent, water charges, mortgage interest payments, structural insurance premiums and ground rent and service charges.

For more information see the appendices to the HBAI reports (e.g. DWP 2002).

Household income is 'equivalised' to take account of variations in household size and composition. The McClements Equivalence Scale is used, as shown below. The relativities are slightly different depending on whether it is the AHC or BHC income concept that is used. For comparison the modified OECD scale is also shown (it has been re-based so that a couple = 1, to make comparisons with the McClements scale easier). The modified OECD scale is commonly used in international comparisons of income distribution and has been adopted as standard by Eurostat. The McClements scale gives a particularly low weight to babies and children aged under 3, relative to the OECD scale.

Equivalised household income is then allocated to each individual within the household and statistics are calculated across individuals. Another way of expressing this is to say that household incomes are weighted by household size. It is implicitly assumed that all individuals within the household share the same living standard (as measured by equivalised income).

Individuals are classified into *family type* and *economic status* (referred to in the text as employment situation) groups according to the status of the benefit unit in which they live. All individuals in a benefit unit are given the same classification.

For family type these are:

- single pensioner: a single adult of state pension age or over
- pensioner couple: a couple where the man is of state pension age or over
- couple with children: a non-pensioner couple with dependent children
- couple without children: a non-pensioner couple with no dependent children
- single with children: a non-pensioner single adult with dependent children
- single without children: a non-pensioner single adult with no dependent children.

For economic status individuals are allocated to the first category which applies in the following order:

- self-employed: benefit units where at least one adult usually is self-employed in their main job for 31 or more hours a week
- single or couple, both in full-time work: benefit units where all adults usually work 31 or more hours a week
- couple, one in full-time work, one in part-time work: benefit units where one partner usually work 31 or more hours a week and the other partner usually works fewer than 31 hours a week

Table A1 Equivalence scale relativities			
	McClements (BHC)	McClements (AHC)	Modified OECD
First adult	0.61	0.55	0.67
Spouse of first adult	0.39	0.45	0.33
Other second adult	0.46	0.45	0.33
Third adult	0.42	0.45	0.33
Fourth + adults	0.36	0.40	0.33
Child aged 0–1	0.09	0.07	0.20
Child aged 2–4	0.18	0.18	0.20
Child aged 5–7	0.21	0.21	0.20
Child aged 8–10	0.23	0.23	0.20
Child aged 11–12	0.25	0.26	0.20
Child aged 13	0.27	0.28	0.20
Child aged 14–15	0.27	0.28	0.33
Child aged 16–18	0.36	0.38	0.33

- couple, one in full-time work, one not working: couples, where one partner usually works 31 or more hours a week and the other partner does not do paid work
- one or more in part-time work: benefit units where at least one adult works, but for fewer than 31 hours a week
- head or spouse unemployed: benefit units where at least one adult is unemployed
- others: benefit units not classified above (this group includes the long-term sick, disabled people and non-working single parents).

■ Appendix II
Decomposing poverty changes

If p_i is the proportion of the population in type i and P_i is the proportion of that type who are poor, then overall poverty, P_{total}, is given by

$$P_{total} = \sum_i p_i.P_i$$

If we distinguish time periods t and t' then

$$P_{total,t} = \sum_i p_{i,t}.P_{i,t}$$

and

$$P_{total,t'} = \sum_i p_{i,t'}.P_{i,t'}$$

The change in poverty is then

$$P_{total,t'} - P_{total,t} = \sum_i p_{i,t'}.P_{i,t'} - \sum_i p_{i,t}.P_{i,t}$$

$$\approx \sum_i (p_{i,t'}-p_{i,t}) \left(\frac{P_{i,t} - \bar{P}_{i,t} + P_{i,t'} - \bar{P}_{i,t'}}{2} \right) + \sum_i \left(\frac{p_{i,t} + p_{i,t'}}{2} \right)(P_{i,t'}-P_{i,t})$$

$$z \qquad \approx \qquad x \qquad\qquad + \qquad\qquad y$$

Thus the overall change in poverty (z) may be divided into that due to compositional changes (x) and that due to changes in the incidence of poverty (y).

Appendix III ■
Policy simulation using POLIMOD

POLIMOD is a tax-benefit microsimulation model constructed and maintained by the Microsimulation Unit in the Department of Applied Economics at the University of Cambridge: see Redmond et al. (1998) for more information. The household income variables used here to measure poverty have been deliberately defined to be as similar as possible to those used in the HBAI statistics and in Chapter 2 of this report. There are some minor departures from HBAI methodology as a result of the fact that we must simulate taxes and benefits (and earnings, where these are affected by the NMW) in order to evaluate changes in the rules that govern them. The 1999/2000 FRS micro-data are updated and backdated to 1997, 2000/1 and 2003/4 levels of prices and incomes in order to evaluate contemporary policy changes, whereas HBAI statistics for a given year use data collected in that year. In addition, there are some differences that arise because some components of income (taxes and benefits) are simulated rather than using values recorded in the survey data.

POLIMOD calculates liabilities for or entitlements to: income tax, National Insurance contributions (NICs), Child Benefit, Family Credit (FC), Working Families Tax Credit (WFTC), Working Tax Credit (WTC), Child Tax Credit (CTC), Income Support (IS) – including income-related Jobseekers Allowance and pensioners' Minimum Income Guarantee – Pension Credit, Housing Benefit (HB) and Council Tax Benefit (CTB). The effect of the minimum wage is modelled by assuming that all with hourly earnings below the relevant minimum are brought up to it and that working hours do not change. Resulting changes in earnings then affect tax and benefits. Otherwise, elements of income are drawn from the recorded values in the FRS dataset. The main effect of simulating the tax and benefit components of income appears to be to narrow the income distribution to some extent.

POLIMOD captures the effects of non-take-up of pre-2003 means-tested benefits (FC/WFTC, IS, HB and CTB) by applying the take-up proportions estimated by the Department of Social Security (DSS 2000). For example we assume that some 20 per cent of lone parents do not receive the FC (or WFTC) to which they are entitled, and 15 per cent of people of working age do not receive the IS to which they are entitled.[20] In general we assume that take-up behaviour is not affected by changes in the size of benefit entitlements. Little is known about what to expect in relation to take-up of the new tax credits, introduced in 2003. We assume that take-up of income-tested CTC will be the same as IS (on a case-by-case basis); take-up of WTC is assumed to be the same as WFTC and to have the same probability for the new groups who are eligible. Take-up of both parts of the Pension Credit (Guarantee Credit and the Savings Credit) is assumed to be the same as that for IS for pensioners.

■ Appendix IV
Modelled changes in tax and benefit policy 1997–2003/4

Changes that are due for implementation part-way through a fiscal year are modelled as though they apply all year.[21]

Amounts are weekly and in current prices and differences are expressed in real terms, unless otherwise specified.

Changes April 1997–2000/1 (October 2000)

The *minimum wage* was introduced in 1999. In 2000/1 the rate for employees aged 22 and over was £3.70 and the rate for young and trainee workers was £3.20.

Lone-parent benefit was abolished (the 1997 benefit would have been worth £6.50 in 2000/1 prices).

Child benefit increased in real terms by £3.25 for first or only children and £0.30 for other children.

Working Families Tax Credit (WFTC) replaced Family Credit in 1999. It had a more generous starting point, a lower taper (55 per cent instead of 70 per cent); a higher adult credit, higher credits for children particularly those aged under 11, but also those aged 11–15 but lower credits for children aged 18. (The Child Care Tax Credit is not modelled.)

Income Support: lone-parent premium abolished (it would have been worth £5.25 in 2000/1); family premium increased by £2.90; rates for children aged under 11 increased by £13.65, for children aged under 16 increased by £4.85; rates for children aged 18 reduced to the under 18 rate. Disability premiums increased slightly.

Housing Benefit (HB) and *Council Tax Benefit* (CTB) changes match those for Income Support except that the real value of the 1997 lone-parent premiums (abolished) is £11.95 in 2000/1 prices.

Minimum Income Guarantee (MIG): the capital limits for MIG (Income Support for pensioners) are increased from £3,000 to £6,000 (so that income from capital less than £6,000 per benefit unit is disregarded) and from £8,000 to £12,000 (so that pensioners with capital between £8,000 and £12,000 may be entitled to MIG assuming other conditions are met). Premiums increased by £5.75 (single) and £9.00 (couples).

Capital thresholds in all means-tested benefits except MIG (and including WFTC) reduced in real value. (These have not been up-rated since 1988.)

Winter fuel allowance: £100 per year for households containing a person over state pension age or in receipt of Income Support pensioner premium.

Incapacity Benefit is reduced by 50p for every £1 of occupational or personal pension income over £85 per week.

National Insurance contributions: Class 1 employee contribution lower earnings limit (LEL) increased by £10 in real terms; upper earnings limit (UEL) increased by £75; contributions on earnings below the LEL ('entry fee') abolished (worth up to £1.62 per week). Class 2 (self-employed) contributions reduced by £4.90. Class 4 (self-employed) lower profits limit aligned with the Class 1 LEL (a reduction of £67); Class 4 upper profits limit aligned with the Class 1 UEL (an increase of £75) and the rate of Class 4 increased from 6 per cent to 7 per cent.

Income tax schedule: introduction of a 10 per cent lower rate; this applies on the first £1,520 (2000/1 prices) of annual taxable income, including income from investments (replaces 20 per cent lower band); standard rate reduced from 23 per cent to 22 per cent.

Married Couples Allowance (MCA) for couples both aged under 65 and *additional personal allowance* for lone parents abolished. (Under 1997 policy these would have been worth 15 per cent of £2,000 per year or £5.77 per week in 2000/1 prices.) Age-related MCA increased so that pensioner couples do not lose. Age-related personal allowances increased.

Mortgage tax relief abolished. (In 1997 the maximum annual relief was 15 per cent of the annual interest on £30,000.)

Council tax increased in real terms by 11 per cent (on average). This represents an increase of about £1.80 per week on a Band D Council Tax in 2000/1 prices.

Changes 2000/1 (October 2000)–2003/4 (October 2003)

The *minimum wage* took the values of £4.20 and £3.60 in October 2002. In 2003/4 prices these are worth £3.93 and £3.37.[22]

Child benefit increased in real terms by £0.05 for all children.

Maternity pay: the flat rate element increased to £100 in 2003/4. This is equivalent to a real increase of £33 per week.

The *Child Tax Credit* and the *Working Tax Credit* replace Working Families Tax Credit and Disabled Persons Tax Credit in 2003/4. The *Child Tax Credit* also subsumes the Children's Tax Credit (see below under income tax) and the child elements of Income Support. The maximum value of this credit involves an increase in rates per child and per family. The credit is tapered away according to the gross income (with a lower taper than in WFTC, which depended on net income) and investment income is included (rather than capital limits and tariff income as in IS and WFTC). The *Working Tax Credit* (WTC) uses similar rules about work conditions as WFTC/DPTC, but extends entitlement to some groups without children or disabilities (working 30+ hours). The Child Care Tax Credit is linked to entitlement to WTC (but is not modelled here).

Income Support: Support for children of families on IS is transferred to the Child Tax Credit. Effective levels of support are increased by £6.05 for children under 15 and £5.20 for older children and the family premium increased by £0.85; premiums for disabled children are increased significantly; disability premiums increased again. The earnings disregard in Income Support and Jobseekers Allowance for lone parents, disabled people and carers increased by £5 to £20 in April 2001.

Housing Benefit (HB) and *Council Tax Benefit* (CTB) changes to rates and premiums match those for Income Support (and the pension credit – see below).

Basic state retirement pension (and widow's pension) increased in real terms by £4.50 (Cat. A) or £2.75 (Cat. B).

The *Pension Credit* (PC) replaces the Minimum Income Guarantee. It has two parts, both of which are assessed jointly for couples: the *Guarantee Credit* (GC), based on MIG but with some relaxation of rules, and the *Savings Credit* (SC) which is an additional top-up for those with modest incomes above the MIG and/or basic pension level. In the GC, for those aged 60+ and their partners the upper capital limit is removed and the assumed tariff rate of income from capital is halved. Hours of work conditions are removed and some sources of income are exempted from the income test. Benefit levels are increased by around 25 per cent in real terms (relative to 2000/1 levels). In addition the *Savings Credit* is for people aged 65+ and their partners. This tops up small amounts of qualifying income above the level of the basic state pension at a rate of 60p per £ of income (assessed jointly), up to a maximum. The SC is reduced by any income in excess of the Guarantee Credit level at a rate of 40 per cent.

Capital thresholds in all means-tested benefits (except the PC upper limit) reduced in real value. (These have not been up-rated since 1988.)

Winter fuel allowance: Increased to £200 per year for households containing a person over state pension age or in receipt of Income Support pensioner premium.

National Insurance contributions: Class 1 employee contribution lower earnings limit (LEL) increased by £8; upper earnings limit (UEL) reduced by £30; Class 1 rate increased from 10 per cent to 11 per cent and extra 1 per cent charged on all earnings above the UEL; *Class 4* (self-employed) rate increased from 7 per cent to 8 per cent and an extra 1 per cent charged on profits above the upper profits limit; this limit reduced in real terms by £30.

Income tax: Age-related personal allowances increased by more than inflation; increase in width of 10p tax band by £300 per year in real terms in 2001; personal allowance not indexed in 2003/4.

Introduction of a *Children's Tax Credit* took place in 2001/2. This is for taxpayer families with children aged under 16. If either parent is a higher rate (40 per cent) taxpayer, the value of the annual credit is tapered at a rate of £1 for every £15 of income per year above the 40 per cent threshold. The credit was introduced at the level of £10.00 per week per eligible taxpaying family (£520 per year). An additional Baby Tax Credit for families with a child born within the year was introduced in 2002/3. This was tapered along with the children's tax credit and took the same maximum value. In 2003/4 these credits become part of the Child Tax Credit (see above).

Council tax increased in real terms by 16 per cent (on average). This represents an increase of about £3.20 per week on a Band D Council Tax in 2003/4 prices.

Appendix V

Summary of methods and adjustment factors used to update (backdate) 1999/2000 FRS monetary variables to 2000/1, 2003/4 and 1997

Item to be updated	To 2000/1	To 2003/4	To 1997
Employee earnings	Adjusted by a quarterly index derived from monthly average earnings index, whole economy, Labour Market Trends, December Table E.1 (The more disaggregated method used for longer term updating is not appropriate for updating by one year.) [Q2 **1.041**; Q3 **1.038**; Q4 **1.042**; Q1 **1.049**]	Disaggregated New Earnings Survey data (from April 1999–April 2001) used to create indices by gender and quantile of the earnings distribution. Adjustment from quarter of interview to April 1999 and from April 2001 to October 2002 use average earnings index. Projection to October 2003 assumes same rate of growth as October 2001–October 2002.	Disaggregated New Earnings Survey data (from April 1999–April 1997) used to create indices by gender and quantile of the earnings distribution. Adjustment from quarter of interview to April 1999 uses average earnings index.
Income from self-employment	Data adjusted from end of accounting year (may be before 1999) to October 1999. Then adjusted by change in average earnings index, whole economy October 1999–October 2000 [**1.0363**]	Data adjusted from end of accounting year (may be before 1999) to October 1999. Then adjusted by change in average earnings index, whole economy October 1999–October 2002 then adjusted to October 2003 assuming same rate of growth. [**1.1465**]	Data adjusted from end of accounting year (may be before 1999) to October 1999. Then adjusted by change in average earnings index, whole economy October 1999–April 1997. [**0.9003**]
Investment income	(1) Capital imputed from income using 1999/2000 interest rate (bank savings rates according to 3 levels of balance) [**1.55%; 4.02%; 4.10%**] (2) Index capital by change in interest income to households and NPISHs (Calculated from: Financial Statistics, November	(1) Capital imputed from income using 1999/2000 interest rate (bank savings rates according to 3 levels of balance) [**1.55%; 4.02%; 4.10%**] (2) Index capital by change in interest income to households and NPISHs (Calculated from: Financial Statistics, December	(1) Capital imputed from income using 1999/2000 interest rate (bank savings rates according to 3 levels of balance) [**1.55%; 4.02%; 4.10%**] (2) Index capital by change in interest income to households and NPISHs (Calculated from: Financial Statistics, December

Item to be updated	To 2000/1	To 2003/4	To 1997
	2001, Table 14.8A, Income and Capital Account: Households and NPISHs NSSH, col. ROYM, interest D.41, seasonally adjusted) **[1.1711]** (3) Re-impute income using 2000/1 interest rates **[1.88%; 4.43%; 4.44%]**	2002, Table 14.8A, Income and Capital Account: Households and NPISHs NSSH, col. ROYM, interest D.41, seasonally adjusted) **[0.8871]** (3) Re-impute income using latest (October 2002) interest rates **[0.52%; 2.35%; 2.49%]**	1998, Table 14.8A, Income and Capital Account: Households and NPISHs NSSH, col. ROYM, interest D.41, seasonally adjusted) [1.0104] (3) Re-impute income using April 1997 interest rates **[2.97%; 4.57%; 4.96%]**
Income from occupational pensions	Change in RPI October 1999–October 2000 **[1.0322]**	Change in RPI October 1999–October 2002 plus projection to October 2003 using 2002 PBR forecast **[1.0980]**	Change in RPI October 1999–April 1997 **[0.9396]**
Income from private pensions	Change in RPI October 1999–October 2000 **[1.0322]**	Change in RPI October 1999–October 2002 plus projection to October 2003 using 2002 PBR forecast **[1.0980]**	Change in RPI October 1999–April 1997 **[0.9396]**
Non means-tested benefits:	Actual change in each benefit (using change in main rate) [changes are around the change in RPI]	Actual change in each benefit (using change in main rate) [changes are around the change in RPI except the basic state pension and maternity benefits, which are larger]	Actual change in each benefit (using change in main rate) [changes are around the change in RPI]
Income from other sources	Change in RPI October 1999–October 2000 **[1.0322]**	Change in RPI October 1999–October 2002 plus projection to October 2003 using 2002 PBR forecast **[1.0980]**	Change in RPI October 1999–April 1997 **[0.9396]**
Student incomes	Change in RPI October 1999–October 2000 **[1.0322]**	Change in RPI October 1999–October 2002 plus projection to Oct 2003 using 2002 PBR forecast **[1.0980]**	Change in RPI October 1999–April 1997 **[0.9396]**
Household rent	Change in RPI (rent) (from September 1999–September 2000) **[1.0315]**	Change in RPI (rent) (from September 1999–September 2002) plus projection to October 2003 using 2002 PBR forecast for all items RPI **[1.1200]**	Change in RPI (rent) (from September 1999–April 1997; mean of September 1996 and September 1997) **[0.9254]**

Item to be updated	To 2000/1	To 2003/4	To 1997
Water charges	Change in RPI (water and other housing payments) (from September 1999–September 2000) **[0.9055]**	Change in RPI (water and other housing payments) from September 1999–September 2002 plus projection to October 2003 using 2002 PBR forecast for all items RPI **[0.9850]**	Change in RPI (water and other housing payments) (from September 1999–April 1997; mean of September 1996 and September 1997) **[0.8871]**
Gross mortgage interest	Change in RPI (mortgage interest payments) (from September 1999–September 2000) **[1.2832]**	(i) Change in total amount outstanding of loans secured on dwellings (Financial Statistics 3.2c) 2000Q3–2002Q3, projected to 2003Q3 using trend growth 2001–2002Q3, multiplied by (ii) change in mortgage interest rate 2000Q3–2002Q3, deflated by (iii) change in MI RPI September 99– September 00 **[1.3073]**	(i) Change in total amount outstanding of loans secured on dwellings (Financial Statistics 3.2c) 2000Q3–1997Q1, multiplied by (ii) change in mortgage interest rate 2000Q3–2002Q3, deflated by (iii) change in MI RPI September 99–September 00 **[0.9922]**
Domestic rates (Northern Ireland only)	Change in RPI October 1999–October 2000 **[1.0322]**	Change in RPI October 1999–October 2002 plus projection to October 2003 using 2002 PBR forecast **[1.0980]**	Change in RPI October 1999–April 1997 **[0.9396]**
Occupational Pension contributions	Average earnings index, whole economy October 1999–October 2000 **[1.0363]**	Average earnings index October 1999–October 2002; projected to October 2003 assuming same rate of growth **[1.1465]**	Average earnings index, whole economy October 1999–April 1997 **[0.9003]**
Council tax (GB only)	Regional index constructed using change in regional average Band D council tax (1999/2000–2000/1) [mean over regions: **1.0622**]	Regional index constructed using change in regional average Band D council tax (1999/2000–2003/4) [mean over regions: **1.3092**]	Regional index constructed using change in regional average Band D council tax (1999/2000–April 1997 [mean over regions: **0.8623**]

Notes ■

1 An earlier version of some parts of this report was included in our interim report (CASE paper 63) published in December 2002. This final report expands and revises some of those findings.

2 The estimates shown here differ from those in Table 9 of Piachaud and Sutherland (2002) because they (a) include real changes in the level of council tax; (b) revise 2003/4 policy parameters following 2002 PBR announcements; and (c) incorporate the Pension Credit into the 2003/4 policy regime.

3 The latest announced increase in National Minimum Wage (NMW), due for introduction in October 2003, has not been included.

4 The PSA target uses 1998/9 as the baseline rather than 1997. Child poverty rates were a little higher in 1996/7 than 1998/9: 34 per cent and 33 per cent respectively on an AHC basis (DSS 1999; DSS 2000).

5 As with the child poverty rates these calculations simply count the number of pensioners living in households with income below the poverty line, without trying to distinguish by family type or the characteristics of other family members.

6 The Pension Credit is modelled as though it is received throughout 2003/4.

7 Median BHC equivalised household income for pensioners is 9.0 per cent higher than the median value for AHC income. The corresponding figure for the whole population is 13.4 per cent.

8 It should be noted that this depends partly on assumptions regarding projections to October 2003 from the most recently available information: see Appendix V.

9 See Sutherland (2002) for a detailed discussion.

10 In its former incarnation as the Department of Social Security. See DSS (2000a).

11 The Treasury (2002: 90) estimated a 1.5 million reduction on a similar basis.

12 This figure of 1.1 million is the same as that estimated by Brewer and Kaplan (2003) using similar assumptions. It is significantly larger than the estimate of 750,000 given in Piachaud and Sutherland (2002). The main reasons for this difference is the more comprehensive coverage of policy changes in the present analysis. The AHC estimates are also affected by a revision in the method of updating and projecting mortgage interest payments. Chapter 4 discusses this further.

13 There are models which predict take-up, but these tend to focus on single benefits for particular client groups (Blundell et al. 1988; Fry and Stark 1987). A comprehensive model which takes account of the (changing) structure of multiple means-tested benefits and complex households containing several benefit units entitled to different benefits does not, to our knowledge, exist.

14 The dimensions controlled for include housing tenure, council tax band, residence in London, age and sex categories for single people and couples and numbers of families with children, with lone parents distinguished by sex.

15 The Family Expenditure Survey covers the United Kingdom, in contrast with the Family Resources Survey which covers Great Britain.

16 Adjustment factors are provided by the ONS: 1.68 for alcohol, 1.81 for tobacco, 1.50 for sweets and confectionery, 1.60 for ice-cream and 1.15 for soft drinks.

17 For standard-rated items, estimated VAT payments are equal to total spending on those items multiplied by 0.175/1.175.

18 Probabilities are the same as those assumed by the Office for National Statistics (ONS) in their Redistribution of Income (ROI) analyses. Their methodology report was kindly provided by the ONS.

19 We do not observe the current value of their home, so this is estimated using another data set, the Family Resources Survey, based on the value of properties with similar characteristics.

20 These were based on FRS and administrative data for 1998/9, before the replacement of FC by WFTC. More recent estimates for WFTC from the summer of 2000 using the Families and Children Survey are provided by McKay (2002). He finds a caseload non-take-up rate of 38 per cent for all families and a rate of 26 per cent for lone parents.

21 For example, the increases in WFTC introduced in mid-2000/1 are modelled as though they applied throughout the year. See Brewer et al. (2002) for a discussion of how WFTC changes affected incomes during the year. The Pension Credit, due for introduction in October 2003, is modelled as though it applied throughout 2003/4.

22 An announcement of an increase in the level of the minimum wage to £4.50 and £3.80 in October 2003 has been made since carrying out the calculations reported here.

References ■

Adam, S. and Kaplan, G. (2002) 'A survey of the UK tax system', IFS Briefing Note No. 9, London: Institute for Fiscal Studies.

Blundell, R., Fry, V. and Walker, I. (1988) 'Modelling the take-up of means-tested benefits: The case of housing benefits in the United Kingdom', *Economic Journal*, 98, 58–74.

Brewer, M., Clark, T. and Goodman, A. (2002) *The Government's child poverty target: How much progress has been made?* London: Institute for Fiscal Studies, Commentary 87.

Brewer, M. and Kaplan, G. (2003) 'What do the child poverty targets mean for the child tax credit?' in R. Chote, C. Emmerson and H. Simpson (eds) *The IFS Green Budget: January 2003*, London: Institute for Fiscal Studies, Commentary No. 92.

Dayal, N., Gomulka, J., Mitton, L., Sutherland, H. and Taylor, R. (2000) 'Enhancing Family Resources Survey income data with expenditure data from the Family Expenditure Survey: Data comparisons', Microsimulation Unit Research Note MU/RN/40, Department of Applied Economics, University of Cambridge.

DSS (Department of Social Security) (1997) *Households Below Average Income: A statistical analysis 1979–1994/95*, London: The Stationery Office.

DSS (Department of Social Security) (1999) *Households Below Average Income, 1996/7*, London: The Stationery Office.

DSS (Department of Social Security) (2000) *Households Below Average Income, 1998/9*, London: The Stationery Office.

DSS (Department of Social Security) (2000a) *Income related benefits: estimates of take-up in 1998–99*, London: DSS Analytical Services Division.

DWP (Department for Work and Pensions) (2002) *Households Below Average Income, 2000/1*, London: The Stationery Office.

DWP (Department for Work and Pensions) (2002a) *Opportunity for all: 4th annual report*, London: The Stationery Office.

DWP (Department for Work and Pensions) (2003) *Households Below Average Income, 2001/2*. London: The Stationery Office.

Frosztega, M. and the Households Below Average Income team (2000) 'Comparisons of income data between the Family Expenditure Survey and the Family Resources Survey', *GSS Methodology Series* No. 18, London: Office for National Statistics.

Fry, V. and Stark, G. (1997) 'The take-up of supplementary benefits: Gaps in the safety net', *Fiscal Studies*, 8, 1–18.

Gardiner, K. and Hills, J. (1999) 'Policy implications of new data on income mobility', *Economic Journal*, 109, F91–F111.

HM Customs and Excise (2003) *Annual Report 2000–2001*, Tables and Statistics, available on-line on the HM Customs and Excise website <www.hmce.gov.uk/about/reports/ann-report-stats.htm>.

HM Treasury (2001) 'Tackling child poverty: giving every child the best possible start in life', Pre-Budget Report Document, December.

HM Treasury (2002) *Budget 2002: The strength to make long term decisions,* HC 592, London: The Stationery Office.

Lakin, C. (2002) 'The effects of taxes and benefits on household income, 2000–01', *Economic Trends,* 582, May.

McKay, S. (2002) *Low/moderate income families in Britain: work, working families tax credit and childcare in 2000,* DWP Research Report No. 161, Corporate Document Services (CDS), Leeds.

McKnight A. (2000) *Trends in earnings inequality and earnings mobility, 1977–1997: The impact of mobility on long term inequality,* London: Department of Trade and Industry, Employment Relations Research Report Series 8.

Piachaud, D. and Sutherland, H. (2001) 'Child poverty in Britain and the new Labour government', *Journal of Social Policy,* 30 (1), 95–118.

Piachaud, D. and Sutherland, H. (2002) *Changing poverty post 1997,* London: Centre for the Analysis of Social Exclusion, London School of Economics, CASE paper 63.

Pudney, S. and Sutherland, H. (1994) 'How reliable are microsimulation results? An analysis of the role of sampling error in a UK tax-benefit model', *Journal of Public Economics,* 53, 327–65.

Redmond, G., Sutherland, H. and Wilson, M. (1998) *The arithmetic of tax and social security reform: A user's guide to microsimulation methods and analysis,* Cambridge: Cambridge University Press.

Sutherland, H. (2002) *One parent families, poverty and Labour policy,* London: National Council for One Parent Families.